1998

ACCOMMODATIONS—
OR JUST
GOOD TEACHING?

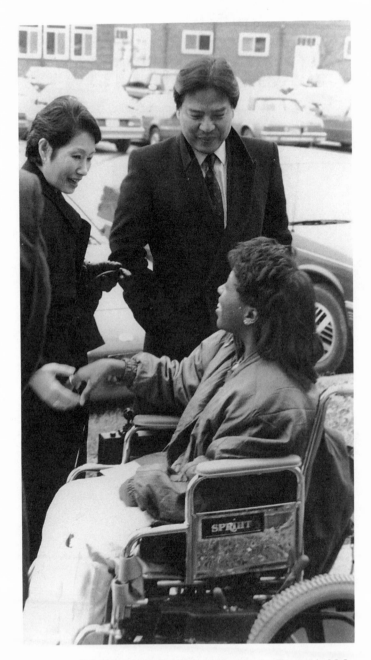

Following a talk at Austin Peay State University, the Honorable M. L. Birabhongse Kasemsri, ambassador of Thailand, and his wife pause a moment to talk with Angela Barksley, an Austin Peay student. Photo by Dennie Burke. Photo courtesy of Austin Peay State University Public Relations and Publications Office. Used with permission.

ACCOMMODATIONS— OR JUST GOOD TEACHING?

Strategies for Teaching College Students with Disabilities

Edited by

BONNIE M. HODGE and JENNIE PRESTON-SABIN

Westport, Connecticut
London

Library of Congress Cataloging-in-Publication Data

Accommodations—or just good teaching? : strategies for teaching
    college students with disabilities / edited by Bonnie M. Hodge,
    Jennie Preston-Sabin.
        p.   cm.
    Includes bibliographical references and index.
    ISBN 0–275–95606–7 (alk. paper)
        1. Handicapped—Education (Higher)—United States.   2. Handicapped
college students—United States.   3. College teaching—United
States.   I. Hodge, Bonnie M.   II. Preston-Sabin, Jennie.
    LC4813.A33   1997
    371.9′0474′0973—dc21   96–37733

British Library Cataloguing in Publication Data is available.

Library of Congress Catalog Card Number: 96–37733
ISBN: 0–275–95606–7

First published in 1997

Praeger Publishers, 88 Post Road West, Westport, CT 06881
An imprint of Greenwood Publishing Group, Inc.

Printed in the United States of America

The paper used in this book complies with the
Permanent Paper Standard issued by the National
Information Standards Organization (Z39.48–1984).

10 9 8 7 6 5 4 3 2 1

Copyright Acknowledgments

The editors and publisher gratefully acknowledge permission to quote
from the following:

Interview with Angela Barksley. Permission to print any or all portions
of the interview granted by Angela Barksley.

For portions from the booklet entitled "A Guide to Reasonable Accommodations" by L. Scott Lissner, published by Longwood College, Virginia. Used with permission.

This book is dedicated to the learner
found in each and every one of us.

CONTENTS

PREFACE

One of the fastest growing populations on the college and university campus today is the student with disabilities. The Rehabilitation Act of 1973, specifically Section 504 regulations, not only increased awareness among educators of the needs of such a diverse population, but has served notice that accommodations must be made to provide equity in education. The Americans with Disabilities Act was passed in 1990, further focusing attention on the needs of students with disabilities. As a result, all American citizens now have the right to expect equal access to higher education. As educators, we are required to implement practical accommodations for these students.

Students with disabilities who began their formal education after 1973 often have academic records that not only document the disability, but also outline those accommodations that have proven successful for that particular student. However, for many of our nontraditional students this documentation simply does not exist. Many of these students are not aware that they may have a disability, let alone that accommodations can be provided to equalize their opportunities for success in the pursuit of their educational goals.

Often students with documented disabilities have been provided accommodations with no idea of how they impact on their learning. In addition, maturation of the student impacts their learning process. Upon entering a postsecondary institution, students with disabilities must be provided opportunities to receive appropriate guidance about their learning needs, and professors and advisors of these students must receive solid support to provide the necessary teaching adjustments for them.

This book is the result of an ongoing project with the goal of identifying teaching strategies and/or accommodations for students with disabilities that have proven practical and successful for teaching practitioners who are not experts in the field of special education or disability issues, but have expertise in good teaching. These strategies and accommodations were compiled from anecdotal subchapters submitted by members of the National Association for Developmental Education. The information provided in this book is invaluable to classroom teachers who are concerned with meeting the individual needs of their students, to supervising teachers who are preparing future classroom teachers, and to the administration and staff who are supporting and providing the network between students with disabilities and their teachers.

It is clear that working with students with disabilities is a rewarding challenge in higher education and the educators of these students are eager to share their experiences. This book has become one way to tap into the rich resources of the practical knowledge of those working daily with students with disabilities so that it can be shared by others. It is easy to see that students, facilitated by caring educators, will benefit most from this knowledge as they continue seeking ways to find their own best path toward learning.

BOOK HIGHLIGHTS

The definition of accommodation is presented.

Legal implications about making an accommodation by faculty members in higher education are presented by L. Scott Lissner, ADA/504 Compliance Officer, Longwood College, Virginia.

Anecdotal subchapters linking good teaching techniques to individual learning needs are provided by thirty-two teaching practitioners in higher education to illustrate how a professor accommodates a student.

Subchapters are grouped by impact areas so that any instructor can easily access pertinent information for their students' learning needs.

Each impact area is accompanied by a checklist of commonly used accommodations for students. This helps instructors by providing a starting point for the investigation of possible teaching adaptations for any given situation that occurs when helping a student with a specific disability.

A coalition model for student success is presented for implementation at postsecondary institutions.

ACKNOWLEDGMENTS

This book represents the culmination of a four-year-long project in which two math instructors looked for practical accommodations for students with disabilities in a traditional classroom, first in the area of mathematics and then into other content areas. The project actually began one day in an office shared by the two math instructors, Bonnie and Jennie. Jennie was elated over the success she was having with a student named Angela Barksley who could finally operate with signed numbers and Bonnie was musing that the process of helping individual students should be less time-consuming for the instructor since resources should readily be available for both student and instructor. One thing led to another and before long, Dr. Carlette Hardin, Director of Developmental Studies at Austin Peay State University, offered advice and assistance to Bonnie and Jennie by encouraging them to apply for the National Association for Developmental Education's (NADE) Professional Development Scholarship Award and for Austin Peay State University's (APSU) Tower Research Fund Award. Both of these helped provide monetary support to conduct a nationwide search for practical strategies and accommodations proven to be successful by teaching practitioners in higher education. Bonnie and Jennie enlisted the support of their families to prepare over 2,000 questionnaires and a call for anecdotal essays directed toward the NADE membership. Blaine Hodge, Trey Hodge, Blaire Hodge, Dave Sabin, Kate Sabin, John Preston, and Winifred Preston helped Bonnie and Jennie to fold, insert, seal, and stamp each questionnaire and envelope. After receiving helpful bulk mailing instructions from APSU's post office manager, Mrs. Sharon Ridenhour, responses poured into Bonnie and Jennie's campus mailboxes. There was a 15% response rate—much higher than the 5% rate that was forecast. The NADE membership affirmed that there is a need for more direct information about students with disabilities available to the professor in higher education.

As the months went by, Bonnie and Jennie contacted respondents and the essays that resulted are now available in this book. During this collecting and sorting phase, presentations were given at the following conferences: 19th Annual NADE Conference, National Institute for Staff and Organizational Development International Conference on Teaching Excellence, Geier Workshop Disabilities Conference, 18th Annual NADE Conference, and Tennessee Association for Developmental Education (TNADE) Fall Conference 1993. At both NADE conferences, Bonnie and Jennie were joined in their presentations by contributors Deann Christianson, Andra Dorlac, Maxine Elmont, Mary Mattson-Scirocco, and Elaine Werner. In addition, many discussions and a formal interview were done with student Angela Barksley, who provided her insights about the effects of the accommodation process. Bonnie and Jennie enlisted expertise in WordPerfect from Andrea Host in APSU's Computer Services and from Keith Baggett, a computer lab assistant who provided invaluable assistance from day to day. Also, Scott Lissner of Longwood College, Virginia, contributed his knowledge on the legal aspects of the accommodation process. He was a necessary and welcome ally in the outcome of this book.

Bonnie and Jennie are grateful that so many opportunities have occurred as a result of their quest for better teaching and that so many people have taken the time to be interested, enthusiastic, and supportive of the project they began. Furthermore, they look forward to hearing of others' teaching and learning successes as the search continues for better ways to teach and serve all students who take part in learning. Comments concerning this book and meeting the needs of students with disabilities can be sent directly to Bonnie M. Hodge and Jennie Preston-Sabin at Austin Peay State University, PO Box 4476, Clarksville, TN, 37044 or hodgeb@apsu02.apsu.edu and sabinj@apsu02.apsu.edu.

ACCOMMODATIONS—
OR JUST
GOOD TEACHING?

Chapter 1
MAKING AN ACCOMMODATION

All professors in higher education now encounter students with disabilities in the "traditional" classroom. For many, it becomes a perplexing situation. The student with a disability may or may not have fully developed the maturity shown by a successful student, and the professor may or may not have the sensitivity, training, or both to interact meaningfully with the student. It is essential for all faculty in higher education to understand that all educators accommodate. Often professors do not recognize it as such when they make learning accommodations for students and, therefore, view the idea of "making an accommodation" as a new teaching methodology. No doubt, with support of colleagues and administration, these same professors who may view the student with a disability as a dilemma can identify times they provided an accommodation but had never labeled it as such. Initially, the professor must understand two precepts: (1) the definition of an accommodation, and (2) the circumstances under which he is responsible for providing accommodations. The following subchapter addresses both of these concerns that are frequently voiced by professors in higher education.

Explaining Learning Disabilities to Colleagues: Treatment and Accommodation
by Bruce Barrett

Like many other educators, I have been asked to assume the task of coordinating services for learning disabled students on our campus. Unlike some others, however, I find this task a bit less intimidating; in a former work "life," I was a psychologist, whose area of specialization was to identify and assemble educational programs for individuals experiencing learning difficulties.

A major part of my present job is explaining the nature of learning disabilities to my colleagues, developing ways to "level the playing field" for our learning disabled students in ways that are acceptable and understandable to professors and administrators, and meeting our legal and ethical obligations to our students. One of the most challenging parts of this task is explaining our institution's legal responsibilities toward our learning disabled students to professors and administrators who have little experience in that field. My colleagues realize that addressing the needs of the learning disabled at the university is a relatively new venture, and most will readily admit they don't know much about dealing with these types of disabilities. A few are quite knowledgeable, others less so, and still others know very little or nothing. Some colleagues have had encounters of various kinds of learning disabled relatives or neighbors; others have heard of PL 94-142 (The Education of the Handicapped Act) and Section 504, or the ADA (Americans with Disabilities Act). Most often, however, the reaction I see, when university personnel are asked to address the needs of the learning disabled, is discomfort or fear. The most common response I hear is: "I can't treat a learning disabled student. I don't know anything about learning disabilities."

At this point, it is usually not going to help matters to tell those worried instructors that they can be held personally liable for refusing to meet the needs of the student. Most instructors are already dedicated to teaching students effectively. Most became instructors because they enjoy teaching; few take pleasure in seeing their students fail. Adding fear to the mix won't help the teacher or the student.

In most cases, instructor fear can be minimized and commitment gained by explaining two important terms to them: *treatment* and *accommodation*.

Treatment is something done *with* the student, and *to* the disability. It is the act of applying some remedy with the purpose of eliminating or relieving the disability. To be maximally effective, treatment should be prescribed and delivered by a specialist in the field of learning disabilities. When one provides treatment, one assumes the disability can be remedied or mitigated.

An *accommodation* is something provided *for* a student. It is an adaptation, designed to help the student display knowledge *around* a learning disability. Accommodations may or may not be designed by specialists, but they can nearly always be delivered by nonspecialists. When one provides an accommodation, the aim is not to remedy or even attempt to mitigate the disability. The purpose of accommodation is simply to allow some means for students to display what they know without the interference of the disability. For example, one wouldn't ask a person who has lost his eyesight to write, in longhand, his feelings about a poem. It would be perfectly appropriate, however, to ask that individual to *verbalize* his thoughts and feelings about the work. The goal in both cases is the same: to find out what the student knows about the poem. However, the *means* for assessing the student's knowledge changes; one method is appropriate and allows us to find out what the student knows, and the other does not. The knowledge inside of the student does not change simply because we change the mode of display. If you or I were asked to provide *treatment* for this student, we would probably express trepidation, and would have to decline, and defer to surgeons who could diagnose and perform an operation that would allow the individual to regain the lost eyesight.

The point of my discussion is this: colleges and schools (grades K–12) operate differently toward the learning disabled, under current interpretations of the laws. Schools are mandated to both treat and accommodate the learning disabled. Colleges and universities are mandated to accommodate. They may choose to treat, if they have the resources and believe treatment to be part of their mission. Much of the fear of my colleagues seems to come from a lack of awareness of the differences between accommodation and treatment. However, much of their anxiety can be overcome by explaining the acts of accommodation and of treatment as being both separate and distinct functions, with schools responsible for both, and colleges and universities presently responsible for accommodation. Once these concepts have been explained and understood, one can begin to work with instructors toward accommodating learning disabled students.

When first working with instructors, I avoid using a great deal of formalistic labels and definitions of the disabilities. Rather, instructors are better able to provide effective accommodations when I provide the name of the disability but then work out the accommodations by outlining the implications of the disability, rather than expanding upon the clinical descriptors. For example, "This student has been diagnosed as being dyslexic. That means he is blind to all of the words printed in books, magazines . . . everything. You have just finished teaching the material to your class for the first exam. Rather than giving this student a printed test, which his blindness prevents him from reading, how else could you test him to discern whether or not he knows the material?" Or, "This student has been diagnosed as dysgraphic. That means she cannot write. Rather than having her write the responses to your essay examination, how else could you test her to find out whether she knows the answers to your essay questions?"

When presented with simulated situations like these, following an explanation of accommodation and treatment, instructors are usually far less intimidated by the challenge of accommodating students with learning disabilities. We have also found that these instructors are subsequently more willing to accept and work with learning disabled students.

Making an accommodation to level the playing field for students with disabilities leads to equity in education, a worthwhile goal for every college and university. Good teaching practices only serve to enhance instruction for all students. Educators are responsible for supporting and guiding all students. For the student with a disability, this will mean that the student must identify himself to the professor with an "appropriate and timely request" for an accommodation. Faculty is not required to bend over backward to meet the needs of students who fail to give adequate notice or information of their accommodation needs. However, faculty is responsible for establishing ongoing communication links within the classroom to inform all students that disability support does exist with proper identification and registration through the appropriate administrative units. In addition, faculty is responsible for providing reasonable accommodations based on recommendations provided by the appropriate administrative office.

Students have needs, whether or not they are due to physical, emotional, or learning disabilities. The role of the good teacher at a college or university is to guide students who are qualified toward realizing their potential. Accommodations for students with disabilities is a part of good teaching and good teaching uses accommodations to meet the individual needs of students.

Chapter 2
LEGAL ISSUES CONCERNING ALL FACULTY IN HIGHER EDUCATION
L. Scott Lissner

SECTION 504, REHABILITATION ACT OF 1973
No otherwise qualified handicapped individual in the United States shall, solely by reason of his handicap, be excluded from participation in, be denied the benefits of, or be subject to discrimination under any program receiving federal financial assistance.

THE AMERICANS WITH DISABILITIES ACT, 1990
The nation's proper goals regarding individuals with disabilities are to assure equality of opportunity, full participation, independent living, and economic self-sufficiency for persons with disabilities.

The two quotations above represent the spirit of federal disability rights law. The philosophical goals of equality, independence, and freedom from discrimination are nearly universally appealing. If the spirit of the law is followed when working with students with disabilities, you will rarely need to ask yourself, "Am I within the *letter* of the law?" This chapter explores how the spirit of the law has been translated into the letter of the law.

The best available research estimates that between 6% and 13% of current college students identify themselves as having a disability. This proportion has at least doubled in the past decade (Henderson, 1991; McGuire, Norlander, & Shaw, 1990; Greene & Zimbler, 1989). As this population has grown, there has been increasing pressure from students, federal legislation, and the courts for colleges and universities to improve access.

During the 1993–1994 academic year, 551 disability discrimination complaints were filed with the Office of Civil Rights (OCR). Within these complaints, 290 different compliance concerns were identified. Roughly one-third of these concerns focused on academic issues such as instructional delivery, testing, and course/degree modifications that involve faculty (Disability Compliance for Higher Education, 1996).

There are many dimensions of access to higher education—recruitment, admissions, campus facilities, student services, cocurricular activities, and, most importantly, instruction. This chapter will provide an overview of faculty rights and responsibilities in providing access for students with disabilities. The chapter is divided into two parts. The first section is a case study modeling the application of the law within an instructional situation. This case is intended to both illustrate the law and to provide a sense for the process. The second section provides a brief review of the key federal legislation and case law upon which the case study was built. The appendices at the back of the book contain resource materials; Appendix A contains key federal legislation, Appendix B addresses the accommodation decision making process, and Appendix C addresses the rights and responsibilities of the institution and the student.

THE ACCOMMODATION PROCESS

Imagine that the semester has just started and a student, who is enrolled in your general education statistics course, comes to you during your first office hour. She introduces herself as Lois and says that she has LD and will need unlimited time on all of her tests. You ask the student if she can explain further so that you can better understand her needs. She says, "It slows me down," and offers no further explanation. You then ask her if she has any documentation that would allow you to better understand her needs.

Lois replies, "Oh yeah, my doctor gave me this," reaches into her knapsack and hands you an inch thick file with "Targus Psycho-Educational Center, Dr. Who—Diagnosis: Diffuse Necrologic Desynchronization" neatly hand written on the outside. You quickly skim through the file and see that it is written technical jargon and legalese. It contains diagnostic test results, information on courses and goals from high school along with a set of recommendations. The recommendations seem to be focused on high school and include tutoring, resource room assistance, untimed testing in the resource room, shortened assignments, and the use of a computer for writing and study skills instruction. The most recent date you see is two years ago.

You then explain to the student that you are not sure what this means and ask her to explain how her learning disability affects her work. She says, "I have to work harder and need extra time and help. My high school counselor told me to bring my file to college to explain it."

1. What do you do at this point? The student clearly has documentation, even though it does not make much sense to you. You know the college has a policy to accommodate students with disabilities, but unlimited time for tests does not seem either practical or reasonable to you. The fact that the student seems to know so little about her own needs makes you wonder if she really belongs in your class, but telling her to withdraw based on so little information does not seem right. You know you need some expert help. You decide to send her to the Disability Support Services Office (DSS). Not every institution will have a DSS office, but *every* institution should have a designated Section 504 or ADA Compliance Officer, since the legislation requires that each institution appoint someone to this position.

You tell Lois that the college has a Disability Support Office to help interpret diagnostic material and identify appropriate accommodations. You have her call and schedule an appointment.

Lois comes back to you the next day with an Access Plan from Disability Support Services. She hands you the plan and then sits down and waits.

You read the plan. It confirms that she has a learning disability resulting from a head injury. The current impact of the disability includes (1) impaired motor coordination that reduces her writing speed; (2) phonological coding deficits that interfere with spelling; (3) increased distractibility; (4) deficits in semantic access that interferes with expressive language; and (5) an increased tendency toward impulsive responses.

The plan includes a list of recommended accommodations: (1) extended time for tests—50% for multiple choice, 75% for short answer, and 100% for essays; (2) the opportunity to respond to multiple choice tests on the question page as opposed to a separate answer sheet; (3) an individual and nondistractive testing room; (4) the use of a word processor for essays; (5) the use of a note taker or a tape recorder during lecture; (6) priority registration; and (7) assignment of lab assistants. The plan concludes with the following statement:

All of the above adaptations may not be needed in any one context and some necessary adaptations may not have been foreseen. Because specific tasks and requirements interact with the student's condition differentially, these recommendations should be reviewed in the context of specific requirements. Students, faculty, or staff may request assistance in reviewing the application of these recommendations to a specific course, program or context at any time.

2. What do you need to do next? While this makes more sense than the file she showed you yesterday, the recommendations are still general and do not seem to be focused on your specific course. So far Lois has not been particularly helpful in explaining things, but the plan stated she had expressive language problems. You decide to review the course requirements with her and see if she responds better to specifics.

As you review the course requirements with the student you start with your homework assignments. Typically you assign twenty problems that are due the next class meeting (the class meets on a Monday, Wednesday, Friday schedule), at which time you review the problems in class. They are graded on a three-point scale: zero points for not turning them in, one point for attempting them, and two points for getting at least half of them correct. Over the semester this equates to a test grade with a maximum of eighty possible points as there are forty assignments.

As you describe the homework, Lois comments, "That's a lot of problems. I don't know if I can do that many in two days!" You remember that her plan said she wrote slowly because of coordination problems and you realize that simply writing out the assigned homework problems is going to take her longer than most students.

You have her copy a solved problem from an example in the book. It takes her about one and a half times as long as you think it would take most people. Your experience tells you that students rarely take more than three hours to complete the twenty problems. You estimate that it might take four to six hours for this student.

3. How might the homework assignments be modified to accommodate Lois' disability? You know that in any assignment there are four or five of each type of problem. You consider the possibility of having Lois complete only three or four of each type to reduce the writing load. You also consider teaching Lois how to use the computer statistics package that you normally introduce late in the course early. You could then have her do one of each type of problem by hand to make sure she could do the computations and then complete the remainder on the computer. For most of the problems she would have to understand the concepts to use the computer.

4. You can always choose to provide an accommodation, but would Lois' difficulty with homework require accommodation? While the simple writing out of problems would take Lois longer than the average student, four to six hours of homework between Monday and Wednesday is more a matter of time management and overall workload. It is likely that a fair number of your students take longer than the anticipated average of three hours.

Continuing to review your course requirements, you turn to your in-class tests. These all require that students work from at least one set of raw data (with no more than ten data points), select and calculate the appropriate statistics, and interpret the results. The tests also have several shorter calculation problems and one short essay, for which you expect a half-page response. You design your tests so that they can be completed in half an hour by students who know the material. Almost all of your students finish the test in the allotted forty-five minutes.

5. Does Lois' disability warrant extended time for the tests? Yes, her difficulties with writing speed would justify extended time. Extended time was recommended in her access plan and you do not want to argue with the in-house experts without a good reason. The plan did not quite mention the type of test you give, but it is more like an essay than the other tests mentioned. You decide on a 100% extension.

You and Lois have reviewed all of the course requirements and the access plan. You feel that she should receive extended test time, take her tests in a quiet, nondistractive environment, and be allowed to share notes with another student. You are not sure how to arrange sharing notes and the scheduling of tests—your tiny office is anything but a nondistractive environment.

6. Who do you call for help in arranging the logistics? This will vary based on how each institution is organized. Typically the DSS office, the Compliance Officer, or the Learning Center would be able to help make these arrangements.

You give all of your students an estimate of their grade during the sixth week of classes. Lois has been attending class regularly with only one absence. She has not been to see you since all the arrangements for accommodations were made. She earned a C on her first test, which she took with accommodations. In reviewing her work you see that she earned the maximum points on the four homework assignments, only one point on the next six, and she did not turn in the last two. On the homework she has earned only fourteen of a possible twenty-four points so you decide that her work merits a D at this time.

The next week Lois comes to your office and says that she needs extended time for the homework as an accommodation. You explain that the amount of actual writing has not increased—in fact, it has gone down—since the first two assignments, and ask, "Has anything changed that affects your writing ability in the past two weeks?" Lois says, "No, the work has gotten harder and I need more time." After about fifteen minutes it is clear that you and Lois are not going to agree.

7. Who do you call to facilitate a resolution? The office that provided the documentation, in this case the Disability Support Services Office should be contacted when conflicts cannot be resolved between the faculty member and the student. Depending on your institution's policies you might call the designated Compliance Officer or need to refer the student to a grievance/appeals process. Both of these should exist since they are specifically called for in the legislation.

The coordinator from DSS comes by and talks to you about the course requirements, the assignments, and asks for a copy of the syllabus. After reviewing your syllabus, the course description, the particular homework assignments, and Lois' documentation, the coordinator meets with you and Lois. He agrees that the assignments have gotten conceptually harder but actually require less physical writing. He suggests that Lois sign up for a tutor for the course and attend a time management workshop at the Learning Center. Lois insists that she needs more time for homework and the coordinator will not approve it. Lois decides to appeal this decision.

8. Who reviews this decision and what accommodations are required during the appeals process? The specific procedure for filing an appeal or grievance will vary from institution to institution. However, some procedure is required by law. During an appeals process the accommodations recommended by the designated person within the institution should be provided, even if these are the accommodations being contested.

Lois' appeal is denied. You are satisfied that your standards and judgment have been validated, particularly since Lois is again turning in her homework on time and generally earning the full two points. You know that she has requested a tutor and are glad things have worked out.

On the next test Lois earns a low C. She comes into your office after the test and asks for a further time extension. She says that on the last test she barely had time to finish and did not have a chance to check her work. You feel that two hours to complete a test that you designed to take thirty minutes is more than enough. You deny the request. The two of you cannot agree so once again you call the coordinator of DSS. He asks to review the two tests with Lois' responses.

After the review the coordinator meets with you and Lois. He points out that the second test does require more lengthy responses and that a number of Lois' errors are based on calculations rather than concepts. The coordinator goes on to say that he believes that the accommodations should be extended to 150%.

You consider the possibility of refusing and filing your own appeal of the coordinator's decision. You explain to the coordinator that while you are not specifically measuring speed, at some point additional time would be ridiculous. There has to be some limit. The coordinator asks you, "In doing your own research, what kinds of time limits exist?" You realize that the answer is probably in weeks—possibly in days for a rush project.

It is apparent that in the context of your own work the additional half hour is reasonable, but you are still concerned and ask, "What if Lois is majoring in a field where speed is more critical than in the type of research I conduct?" The coordinator responds by pointing out that those majors will have courses where fluency is central to the course if it is a critical skill for the field. In those courses extended time would not be an appropriate accommodation.

You can see the distinction between the goal of your course and that of a course required in a specific field. You also realize that extra time to stare at the test does not help the student who does not know the material. If Lois does not know the material, more time is not going to make the answers appear in her head, so you agree to the time extension.

This scenario was a positive but realistic look at the give and take that should exist in the accommodation process. While it focused primarily on testing accommodations, the same process could be applied to any other request. Students, particularly new students, have not yet learned either their own limits or the limits to reasonable accommodations. They are adjusting to both the new academic challenges that college presents and to a new set of rights and responsibilities concerning accommodations. As a faculty member you can set the tone for the accommodation process to be a learning process.

When instructors convey that they feel that the accommodation process is an imposition and that they would rather not be bothered, the process will often become adversarial. However, when instructors encourage students to identify themselves, discuss their needs, and take the time to explain the limits inherent in the course's goals, the accommodation process becomes a cooperative problem-solving effort that best captures the spirit of the law.

The next section of this chapter provides the legal parameters that shaped the case study above. As you read the next section you may want to refer back to the case study.

LEGAL REVIEW

A full review of the legal issues surrounding students with disabilities in higher education is beyond the scope of this chapter. This chapter will place the legislation in context by highlighting the key elements of the legislation and case law as they relate to instructional issues. There are two caveats that the reader should bear in mind. First, federal law sets a minimum standard. State law or institutional policy may set a higher obligation of access. You will want to supplement this review with an examination of state law and institutional policy.

Second, Congress was intentionally ambiguous in its choice of terms, such as "otherwise qualified," "reasonable accommodation," and "undue hardship." While this ambiguity is intended to allow local decision making to be based on case-by-case facts and contexts, it has also contributed to confusion. In essence, what the law proscribes is discrimination; what it prescribes is a process for accommodation decision making that attempts to balance the competing rights of students and institutions. Academic modifications truly test the balance between a college's right to maintain the academic and technical standards integral to its mission and the rights of students with disabilities to equal access.

Legislative History

Before examining the legislation that governs higher education, a few comments are necessary concerning The Education of the Handicapped Act (PL 94-142), which was signed into law in 1975. In 1990 this law was superseded by IDEA (The Individuals with Disabilities Education Act, PL 101-476). This law requires that states provide a free and appropriate education in the least restrictive environment possible to children with disabilities between the ages of three and twenty-one. While this legislation focuses on primary and secondary education it impacts higher education. It has influenced the college aspirations and attendance rates of students with disabilities.

Beyond its influence on college aspirations, IDEA shapes the accommodation expectations that students bring to college. Under IDEA, educational goals and standards are adjusted to the student's ability; the educational institution or parents initiate the process and specific funding is provided to support accommodation efforts (NICHY, 1991). These realities are in sharp contrast to the legislation governing higher education.

Section 504 of the Rehabilitation Act

Nearly twenty-five years ago landmark legislation, Section 504 of the Rehabilitation Act of 1973, was enacted. Subpart E of the act was designed to insure that individuals with disabilities had access to higher education. As civil rights legislation, Section 504's intent is similar to that of Title VI of the Civil Rights Act of 1964, and Title IX of the Education Amendments of 1972, which provided protection on the basis of race and sex (Beihl, 1978; Kramer and Dorman, 1990). Under Section 504, individuals with disabilities are protected from exclusion, disparate treatment, and harassment on the basis of their disability.

In terms of the popular analogy of the day, Section 504 sought to add "disability blind" to the "color blind" and "gender blind" society that earlier legislation attempted to create (Percy, 1989; Federal Register, 1989). The goal was stereotype-free decisions based on individual abilities, not assumptions about the impact of individual disabilities.

In developing the original regulatory guidelines for Section 504, the Office of Civil Rights (OCR) of the Department of Health, Education, and Welfare recognized that because of the impact of their disabilities identical treatment might result in discrimination. It would do no good for a college to be "blind" to a student's use of a wheelchair and schedule him or her in rooms that were inaccessible; interpreters are not provided to hearing students but a lecture would be meaningless to a student who is deaf without one. To address this issue the protections of Section 504 were extended to include reasonable accommodations for the impact of a disability (West, 1993; Heyward, 1992; Percy, 1989; Federal Register, 1989).

The legislation above (and the regulations issued under it) guarantees the right of entrance for qualified students with disabilities into our nation's colleges and universities. It further guarantees that once admitted "reasonable" modifications to all aspects of the program that are not "fundamental" or "essential" will be provided, as necessary, to insure an equal educational opportunity. The regulations go on to list specific activities that must be operated in a nondiscriminatory fashion. This list includes, but is not limited to, recruitment, admission, academic programs, extracurricular (student life) programs, housing, financial aid, student employment, support services (counseling, career placement, tutoring), physical education, athletics, recreation, and transportation. The regulations also require that each institution appoint a compliance officer and establish grievance procedures (34 CFR 104). Appendix A presents a summary of the key legislative requirements relevant to student access to higher education.

The Americans with Disabilities Act of 1990

The Section 504 regulations became law in 1978 (Percy, 1989). Since that time they have been refined by case law and reinforced by the ADA. For higher education the ADA had little direct legal impact (Appendix A provides a summary of the general requirements of the ADA). It extended coverage to those few institutions not receiving any federal funds, it required that state institutions develop transition plans to ensure implementation of the ADA, and it provided new guidelines for telecommunications and transportation services (Kramer and Dorman, 1990).

Further supporting the interpretation that the ADA holds higher education to the existing standards of Section 504 is a 1992 memorandum by the Department of Justice (DOJ), the coordinating agency for the ADA. The DOJ memorandum advised the Department of Education's OCR that ADA complaints by students against colleges and universities will be processed first by the OCR under Section 504. If the OCR does not resolve the complaint, the DOJ will then review the complaint under the ADA. The memorandum explains this policy is based on the Department of Justice's analysis that the ADA is closely modeled after Section 504, which has more detailed regulatory guidelines and an established case law (Colker, 1995).

The most significant impact of the ADA has been its influence on public awareness. Since the new aspects of the ADA focus on nondiscrimination and accommodations in private sector employment, more students are viewing higher education as a means to employment. Participation rates by students with disabilities have risen and these students are more aware of their legal right to accommodations. As evidence of this increased awareness, the number of complaints filed with the OCR has been rising since 1990. Between October 1, 1993, and September 30, 1994, 551 disability-based discrimination complaints against postsecondary institutions were filed with the OCR. In 173 of these complaints the OCR found that the colleges investigated were not in full compliance (Disability Compliance for Higher Education, 1996).

Application of Section 504 and the ADA

The brief history above provides a foundation for examining specific requirements of Section 504 and the ADA as they relate to faculty within higher education. The examination below is not meant to be inclusive but to provide a basis for faculty to view requests from students with disabilities. There are three basic questions guiding this section: (1) Who is protected? (2) What is protected? and (3) How should requests be evaluated?

Legal Definition: Who Is Protected?

Generally, faculty will not be asked to evaluate whether or not a student making a request has a disability. However, it is important that they have an understanding of the legal definition of disability. The legal definition of individuals with disabilities is seemingly straightforward (Federal Regulations 29 C.F.R. Part 1630.2g):

(g) Disability means, with respect to an individual—
(1) a physical or mental impairment that substantially limits one or more of the major life activities of such individual;
(2) a record of such an impairment; or
(3) being regarded as having such an impairment.

The definition becomes complex in terms of defining the terms "major life activities" and "substantially limits" used in the first prong of the definition. Before examining this prong let us quickly explore the second and third prongs of the definition.

These two prongs are firmly rooted in prior civil rights legislation based on race and gender. If a student has a record of an impairment or is perceived as having an impairment then they are entitled to protection. These two prongs of the definition are meant to protect individuals from discriminatory treatment based on assumptions about perceived category membership. As earlier laws attempted to eliminate race based decisions, these two prongs are specifically meant to eliminate arbitrary disability-based decisions.

In other civil rights legislation discrimination is clearly "in the eye of the beholder." The perception that an individual belongs to a particular ethnic or racial group (regardless of actual membership) requires stereotype-free decision making. In the context of disability, discrimination can exist in the environment as well as in stereotypical assumptions held by decision makers. In order to provide equitable treatment there are instances where the disability must be taken into account. This reality created the need for the first prong, which provides a legal definition of disability; a physical or mental impairment that substantially limits one or more major life activities.

In defining disability, Congress refused to provide laundry lists of specific conditions. The regulatory agencies responsible for enforcement have followed the congressional lead by providing guidelines and requiring individual case-by-case evaluations. This same approach is used in evaluating requests for accommodations (U.S. Equal Employment Opportunity Commission & U.S. Department of Justice, 1991).

Major life activities are the basic activities that the average person can perform with little or no difficulty. These activities include, but are not limited to, walking, seeing, learning, working, performing manual tasks, speaking, and hearing (U.S. Equal Employment Opportunity Commission & U.S. Department of Justice, 1991).

Individuals are substantially limited if they are unable to perform or are significantly restricted in their ability to perform a major life activity because of the impact of an impairment. Factors that should be considered in making this decision include the nature and severity of the impairment, the duration or expected duration of the impairment, and the long-term impact of the impairment (U.S. Equal Employment Opportunity Commission & U.S. Department of Justice, 1991).

Critical to the above definitions is the concept that an impairment itself is not a disability. It is the interaction of the impact of an impairment and the demands of the environment that create disability. Faculty will not generally be called on to evaluate an impairment, but may be asked to contribute information on the demands of the context.

If a student has a disability in the legal sense, the next question is "Are they 'otherwise qualified'?" An individual with a disability is considered "otherwise qualified" under two conditions. If the individual meets the eligibility criteria for the program, course or services without reasonable accommodations or if, given reasonable accommodations, the individual meets the eligibility criteria for the program, course, or service (*Southeastern Community College v. Davis*, 1979). A refusal on the basis that a student does not possess the qualifications for participation is legitimate. Neither Section 504 nor the ADA require changes in essential or fundamental standards.

What Is Protected?

Section 504 and the ADA offer two levels of protection; nondiscrimination and accommodation. As mentioned above, the first level of protection, nondiscrimination, closely follows previous civil rights laws.

In a case involving the readmission of a law school student, the federal appellate court stated:

Just as Title VII of the Civil Rights Act of 1964 ensures only equal treatment and not "correct" decisions, the Rehabilitation Act requires only stereotype-free assessment of the person's abilities and prospects rather than a correct decision. (*Anderson v. the University of Wisconsin*, 1988)

This short quotation touches on three critical interpretations of Section 504's requirements. First, that decisions cannot be based on stereotypical assumptions concerning a person's disability. Second, it reinforces the need to conduct an individual assessment of a person's abilities. Finally, the court recognized that the correctness of a decision was subjective and influenced by institutional context. The court viewed the law as requiring a nondiscriminatory process, not a particular conclusion.

The second level of protection is the requirement to make modifications in programs, courses, and services. Modifying existing practices and procedures are meant to reduce the impact of a "substantial limitation" resulting from impairments. Therefore this level of protection is extended only to individuals who meet the legal definition for having a disability.

Appendix A includes a summary of Section 504, Subpart E, which lists the requirements for modifications placed on postsecondary educational institutions. Most relevant to faculty are the modifications mentioned under "Academic Adjustments." This list specifically mentions: (a) course substitutions; (b) extensions of time limits for degree completion; (c) modifying the manner in which courses are conducted; (d) modifications to course examinations; (e) the provision of taped texts, sign language interpreters, and readers in libraries; and (f) adapting classroom and laboratory equipment. Limits to modifications that are mentioned include "essential academic requirements" and individually prescribed aids or equipment for personal use or independent study (34 CFR Part 104.44).

While the legislation uses the term "modifications," the courts have borrowed the term "reasonable accommodation" from the employment provisions of Section 504. The first major Section 504 case involving higher education was heard by the Supreme Court in 1979. The case involved a nursing student who was deaf and was requesting that the required surgical nursing rotation be modified or waived. The Court supported the institution's refusal of the request on the grounds that it would substantially alter the program. However, the decision emphasized the need to review requests on a case-by-case basis and the importance of considering new approaches.

We do not suggest that the line between lawful refusal to extend affirmative action and illegal discrimination against handicapped persons always will be clear. It is possible to envision situations where an insistence on continuing past requirements and practices might arbitrarily deprive genuinely qualified handicapped persons of the opportunity to participate in a covered program. Technological advances can be expected to enhance opportunities to rehabilitate the handicapped or otherwise qualify them for some useful employment. Such advances also may enable the attainment of these goals without imposing undue financial and administrative burdens upon a state. Thus situations may arise where a refusal to modify an existing program might become unreasonable and discriminatory. (*Southeastern Community College v. Davis*, 1979)

The Court also provided the following statement on determining if a student with a disability were otherwise qualified: "An otherwise qualified person is one who is able to meet all of a program's requirements in spite of his handicap." (*Southeastern Community College v. Davis*, 1979). Over the next six years the lower courts interpreted the above statement literally, without considering the potential of reasonable modifications, adaptive technology, or auxiliary aids. In 1985 the Supreme Court clarified its meaning:

Davis thus struck a balance between the statutory rights of the handicapped to be integrated into society and the legitimate interest of federal grantees in preserving the integrity of their programs; while a grantee need not be required to make "fundamental" or "substantial" modifications to accommodate the handicapped, it may be required to make "reasonable" ones.

The balance struck in Davis requires that an otherwise qualified handicapped individual must be provided with meaningful access to the benefit that the grantee offers. The benefit itself, of course, cannot be defined in a way that effectively denies otherwise qualified handicapped individuals the meaningful access to which they are entitled; to assure meaningful access, reasonable accommodations in the grantee's program or benefit may have to be made. (*Alexander v. Choate*, 1985)

The two cases above provide a working definition of accommodations within the academic context. Accommodations include the use of auxiliary aids, alternate media, alternate evaluation methods, and modifications to policies and procedures (including instructional delivery and program requirements) that serve to lessen or ameliorate the impact of a disability on eligibility decisions, performance, evaluation, or the ability to benefit from courses, programs, and services. Modifications are considered unreasonable if they would fundamentally alter demonstrable academic or technical standards, substantially alter the nature of the benefit received from the course, program, or service, or present an undue hardship on the institution.

The working definition of reasonable accommodations in an academic context offered above is either flexible or vague, depending on your perspective. It is flexible in that it can be applied to individual cases in context, allowing decisions to be made based on the facts. It is vague and unsatisfying if you hope to find a simple formula for accommodating a student with a particular disability. Because of the tremendous variation that exists in both the impact of disabilities and institutional and course goals, the only constant in the accommodation equation is the process.

An extensive review of the case law does not yield a simple accommodation formula, but does define a process by which to consider requests for accommodation. In the next section the elements of this process will be reviewed.

How Should Requests Be Evaluated?

Before evaluating a request for accommodations, a request must be received. It is clearly the student's responsibility to self-identify, make requests, and provide documentation (*Nathanson v. Medical College of Pennsylvania*, 1991; Lewis and Clark College, 1995). Institutional policies on self-identification and accommodation requests vary. While faculty are not usually responsible for this process, they are often a student's first contact point. Faculty need to be aware of institutional policy and where to refer the student to initiate the documentation and accommodation process.

Once a request is received and documented, the next step is to review the request in context. There are two court cases that provide guidance for the review process. The first case, *Wynne v. Tufts University Medical School* (1991), involved a student's request for an alternate test format. The faculty member, dean, and president at Tufts submitted affidavits testifying that providing an alternative to multiple choice testing in an organic chemistry course had never been done and would, in their professional opinion, undermine the academic integrity and fundamental goals of the course.

In a summary judgment the lower court agreed with the institution. The student appealed. In reviewing the lower court decision, the federal appellate court stated:

First, as we have noted there is a real obligation on the academic institution to seek suitable means of reasonably accommodating a handicapped person and to submit a factual record indicating that it conscientiously carried out this statutory obligation. Second, the Ewing formulation, hinging judicial override on a "substantial departure from the accepted academic norms," is not necessarily a helpful test in assessing whether professional judgment has been exercised in exploring reasonable alternatives for accommodating a handicapped person. We say this because such alternatives may involve new approaches or devices quite beyond accepted academic norms.

There is no mention of any consideration of possible alternatives, nor reference to any discussion of the unique qualities of multiple choice examinations. There is no indication of who took part in the decision or when it was made. Were the simple conclusory averment of the head of an institution suffice, there would be no way of ascertaining whether the institution had made a professional effort to evaluate possible ways of accommodating a handicapped student or had simply embraced what was most convenient for faculty and administration. (*Wynne v. Tufts University School of Medicine*, 1991)

The appellate court remanded the case back to the lower court for trial judgment. Ultimately, Tufts won the case that given their program, there were no reasonable alternatives to the type of multiple choice testing used in the course.

Regardless of the ultimate outcome, the appellate court's decision provides significant guidance in reviewing an accommodation request. Decisions must be based on a real exploration of alternatives. Relying on tradition, common practice, or singular professional judgment will not suffice.

The second case offering guidance, *Pandazides v. Virginia Board of Education* (1991), involved a college graduate who had requested accommodations for the Communication Skills Battery of the National Teachers Examination (NTE). She asked the Virginia Board of Education to waive this requirement for licensure (and hence employment) on the basis of a learning disability. She offered her performance evaluations from student teaching and those evaluations obtained while working in the classroom on probationary status as an alternative measure of her skills and ability. The state denied her the waiver.

The district court found for the state and the student appealed. The federal appellate court negated the district court's judgment for the state and remanded issue for a finding of fact with the following guidance:

Otherwise qualified may be understood more in terms of the job rather than an arbitrary set of requirements. Therefore, the trial court must do more than simply determine whether or not Pandazides meets all the stipulated requirements of the board, but looks to what the position she seeks actually requires.

Accordingly, defendants cannot merely mechanically invoke any set of requirements and pronounce the handicapped applicant or prospective employee not otherwise qualified. The district court must look behind the qualifications. To do otherwise reduces the term "otherwise qualified" and any arbitrary set of requirements to a tautology. (*Pandazides v. Virginia Board of Education*, 1991)

The Pandazides case guides decision makers to look beyond the specific requirement to the underlying purpose of the requirement. The courts have made it clear that one cannot defend a requirement on the grounds that it is a requirement. For example, at Status Quo University there is a foreign language requirement for the bachelor of arts (BA) degree. A student with a documented disability clearly impacting language acquisition asks for the requirement to be waived or substituted as an accommodation. In order to make the decision you have to ask, "Why do we have this requirement?"

While "Good schools do," "It's what makes a BA a BA," or "It has always been this way," are common responses, they would not suffice. The question becomes "What skills, knowledge, and abilities does meeting this requirement represent? How are they related to the student's program?" and "Is there an alternative way for the student to demonstrate them?" You could ask the same questions about why a test is limited to a one-hour period, or why a laboratory experience is part of an introductory chemistry course.

In short, these court cases provide a framework that institutions can use in making accommodation decisions. If called upon to justify a decision, an institution must be able to document the rational relationship of the standard to a student's academic program, the expertise that was brought to bear in searching for reasonable accommodations, and the manner in which the denied accommodations would either fundamentally alter the academic program in question or present the institution with an undue hardship. Summary guidelines for the accommodation decision making process are provided in Appendix B.

Before concluding, there are two more issues surrounding accommodations that need exploration: (1) the individual or office responsible for providing accommodations; and (2) the definition of undue hardship.

The legislation makes the obligation to accommodate an individual institutional. Other than requiring that a compliance officer be designated and a grievance process established, the legislation leaves the allocation of responsibility to the institutions. Most institutions have some support for evaluating requests and student documentation. Typically a central office has been designated to arrange interpreters, taped texts, and adaptive equipment. Less often a central office oversees accommodated testing and arranges for adaptive laboratory equipment. Institutional policy establishes who is responsible for which aspects of implementing accommodations. Regardless of specific policy, faculty are responsible for allowing reasonable accommodations within their courses.

Dinsmore v. Pugh, a suit involving the refusal of a faculty member to allow an accommodation on the grounds of academic freedom, demonstrates faculty responsibility (Newmeyer, 1993; Heyward, 1992; Heyward, Lawton, and Associates, 1991). At the University of California, Berkeley, a mathematics faculty member disagreed with allowing extended time on tests for a student with a learning disability. The disability had been documented and the accommodation approved by the designated person within the university. The faculty member refused claiming that (a) he did not believe there was such a thing as a learning disability; (b) it was unfair to the other students in the course; and (c) academic freedom allowed him to test as he deemed necessary.

The institution had no grievance procedure in place to cover such a dispute, however a series of attempts were made by the administration to explain the need for the accommodation. The administration supported the accommodation and began developing a formal policy to settle such disputes in the future. The faculty member stood his ground and the student filed suit against the faculty member for violating his civil rights. The suit was placed on the court docket but the faculty member settled before it went to trial. There was a nondisclosure agreement binding on both parties to the suit. All that is known is that the student was satisfied and dropped the suit (Heyward, 1992).

The final issue to be addressed in this review is undue hardship. Undue hardship has two aspects, cost and administration. A 1990 appellate court case, *U.S. of America v. the University of Alabama* (1990), addressed some of the undue hardship issues.

Based on an unresolved Office of Civil Rights complaint under Section 504 of the Rehabilitation Act, a suit was filed against the University of Alabama on four issues: a financial needs test in requesting auxiliary aids, the refusal to extend auxiliary aids and accommodations to noncredit/nondegree students, the inaccessibility of the transportation system, and the fact that a separate lab and restricted hours of access to the pool were discriminatory. The appellate court held against the University of Alabama on all four counts.

Two significant aspects of the court's decisions are that all students—whether part time, nondegree or noncredit—are protected by the Rehabilitation Act and that the ultimate financial burden for auxiliary aids is held by the institution. The court declared that the institution may work with a student to seek funding through state vocational rehabilitation services and/or private sources, but if those funds are not available, the institution must assume the cost for auxiliary aids. This obligation is limited by two statements in the legislation. The institution is not obligated to provide auxiliary aids for personal use.

(2) Auxiliary aids may include taped texts, interpreters or other effective methods of making orally delivered materials available to students with hearing impairments, readers in libraries for students with visual impairments, classroom equipment adapted for use by students with manual impairments, and other similar services and actions. Recipients need not provide attendants, individually prescribed devices, readers for personal use or study, or other devices or services of a personal nature. (34 CFR 104)

The second limit on this obligation is undue hardship on the institution. The legislation provides the following guidance on determining undue hardship:

(c) In determining pursuant to paragraph (a) of this section whether an accommodation would impose an undue hardship on the operation of a recipient's program factors to be considered include:
　(1) The overall size of the recipient's program with respect to number of employees, number and type of facilities, and size of budget;
　(2) The type of recipient's operation, including the composition and structure of the recipient's workforce; and
　(3) The nature and cost of the accommodation needed. (34 CFR 104)

From a cost perspective, hardship is based on the institution's budget, not on that of an individual department or office. Given this fact it is unlikely that many academic accommodations will meet this standard.

As we have seen, the concept of accommodation is complex, even when limited to issues relevant to teaching or taking a course. In the face of this complexity, it is important to remember that the purpose of these modifications is to allow a student with a disability an equal opportunity to participate in and benefit from the course. Accommodations are not modifications to the fundamental or essential skills and knowledge being taught or a guarantee of success for the student being accommodated. Put simply, the goal of a course accommodation is to allow the student an equal chance to achieve the purpose of the course. Appendix C provides a summary of the legal requirements of Section 504 and the ADA formatted as a list of institutional and student rights and responsibilities.

REFERENCES

Alexander v. Choate. (1985) 105 S. Ct. 712.

Anderson v. the University of Wisconsin. (1988). 841 F.2d. 737.

Beihl, Richard G. (1978). *Guide to the Section 504 Self-Evaluation for Colleges and Universities.* Washington, DC: National Association of College and University Business Officers.

Berkowitz, E. D. (1987). *Disabled Policy: America's Programs for the Handicapped.* New York: Cambridge University Press.

C.F.R. (1991). Code of Federal Regulation. Washington, DC: U.S. Government Printing Office. Various entries.

Colker, R. (1995). *The Law of Disability Discrimination.* Cincinnati, OH: Anderson Publishing Co.

Disability Compliance for Higher Education. (1996). "OCR finds 'Compliance Concerns' at 173 Schools." Vol. 1, Issue 10.

Federal Register. (1989). 42, Federal Register, 20296.

Greene, B. & Zimbler, L. (1989). *Profile of Handicapped Students in Postsecondary Education. (1987).* Document No. CS 89-337. Washington, DC: National Center for Education Statistics, U.S. Department of Education.

Henderson, C. (1991). *College Freshmen with Disabilities: A Statistical Profile.* Washington, DC: American Council on Education.

Heyward, S. M. (1992). *Access to Education for the Disabled: A Guide to Compliance with Section 504 of the Rehabilitation Act of 1973.* Jefferson, NC: McFarland & Company.

Heyward, Lawton, and Associates (1991). "Provision of Academic Accommodations: Can Faculty Members Be Held Personally Liable for Failure to Accommodate Disabled Students?" *Disability Accommodation Digest,* 1(1), 1, 4.

Jarrow, J. E. (1992). *Subpart E: The Impact of Section 504 on Postsecondary Education.* Columbus, OH: AHEAD.

Jarrow, J. E. (1993). *Title by Title: The ADA's Impact on Higher Education.* Columbus, OH: AHEAD.

Kramer, Saul G. & Dorman, Ann B. (1990). "Colleges and Universities: A White Paper on the Americans with Disabilities Act." New York: Proskauer, Rose Goetz & Mendelsohn.

Lewis and Clark College. (1995). 5 NDLR 261.

McGuire, Joan M., Norlander, Kay A. & Shaw, Stan F. (1990). "Postsecondary Education for Students with Learning Disabilities: Forecasting Challenges for the Future." *Learning Disabilities Focus,* 5(2), 69–74.

Nathanson v. Medical College of Pennsylvania (1991). 926 F.2d. 1368.

Newmeyer, Ward. (1993). Personal Communication from Ward Newmeyer, ADA/504 Compliance Officer at the University of California, Berkeley. 8/09/93.

NICHY (1991). "Post-Secondary Education and Training Opportunities." *Transition Summary,* (7), September, 15–19.

Pandazides v. Virginia Board of Education. (1991). 946 F. 2d. 345.

Percy, S. L. (1989). *Disability, Civil Rights, and Public Policy: The Politics of Implementation.* Tuscaloosa: The University of Alabama Press.

P.L. #93-112, The Rehabilitation Act of 1973. 29 U.S.C. 791, 1991.

P.L. #94-142, The Education of All Handicapped Children Act of 1975. 20 U.S.C. 1400, 1988.

P.L. #101-336, The Americans with Disabilities Act. 42 U.S.C. 12101, 1991.

P.L. #101-476, The Individuals with Disabilities Education Act of 1991. 42 U.S.C. 12200, 1991.

Southeastern Community College v. Davis. (1979). 442 U.S. 406.

U.S. Equal Employment Opportunity Commission and U.S. Department of Justice (1991). *Americans with Disabilities Act Handbook*. Washington, DC: U.S. Government Printing Office.

U.S. of America v. the University of Alabama. (1990). 908 F. 2d. 740.

West, J. (1993). *The Evolution of Disability Rights in Implementing the Americans with Disabilities Act*. Gostin, L. O. and Beyer, H. A. (eds.). Baltimore, MD: Paul H. Brooks Publishing.

Wynne v. Tufts University Medical School. (1991). 932 R. 2d. 19.

Chapter 3
INTEGRATING REASONABLE ACCOMMODATIONS AS A PART OF GOOD TEACHING

Each semester, professors in higher education have the responsibility to establish good communication links as the foundation to building learning independence for students. As more and more students with disabilities access higher learning, these responsibilities will mean increasing demands for good teaching for all students.

This book of teaching strategies and accommodations has been written to address the teaching needs of professors in higher education faced with the learning needs of students with disabilities. Chapters 4 through 11 contain a diverse collection of anecdotal subchapters written by college and university educators who practice good teaching. As part of their good teaching, they assist students with disabilities toward successful course completion in pursuit of degree completion. They do this by allowing the student to make appropriate adaptations through knowledge of his or her learning strengths or, in other words, "making a reasonable accommodation" for the student to become a systematic learner. The guidance exhibited by each author in these anecdotal subchapters is part of his or her good teaching practices for all students.

Chickering and Gamson (1987) summarize these good teaching practices below.

It is apparent that the "reasonable accommodations" that are illustrated in these subchapters are in accordance with these practices.

Seven Principles for Good Practice in Undergraduate Education
1. Good Practice Encourages Student-Faculty Contact
2. Good Practice Encourages Cooperation Among Students
3. Good Practice Encourages Active Learning
4. Good Practice Gives Prompt Feedback
5. Good Practice Emphasizes Time on Task
6. Good Practice Communicates High Expectations
7. Good Practice Respects Diverse Talents and Ways of Learning

It is undisputed that good teaching practices enhance all student learning. For students with disabilities, they may very well be the essential links that connect them to learning independence, life-time achievement, self-reliance, and increased self-confidence.

The interfacing found between students with disabilities and their academic success in college is the continuous interaction they have with their professors, supported by a united administrative organization that promotes academic networking. Such interaction is an essential dimension of access to higher education.

The interview passage that follows contains edited excerpts that were taken from, "An Interview with Angela Barksley" (Hodge & Preston-Sabin, 1994) in preparation for a workshop presentation about teaching students with disabilities. Miss Barksley has cerebral palsy, which has required adaptations to minimize the impact arising from impairments to gross motor mobility, fine motor skills, and eye-hand coordination. The interview took place during her third year at college. In her first two years of college, she had successfully completed the mathematics prerequisites needed to enroll in College Algebra, college core requirements like Fundamentals of Public Speaking, and foundation courses for her major in social work like Introduction to Sociology. Miss Barksley's comments show that communication and caring were most important in the development of her educational goals. Her disability impacted her mathematics learning, but through knowledge of her learning strengths and her self-confidence, academic achievement in mathematics became possible.

Interviewer: During your first semester at college, what challenges did you face?

Miss Barksley: My first semester, I faced many challenges. The first was being able to get around campus. Having walked all during high school, I never had to worry about being confined to a chair or getting to class on time or having to carry books but I decided to get a chair or something that would help me to get around and it's been a great asset. Having the math disability that was not noted until my second semester, I had to say, "Hi, I can't understand this and I need a little bit of extra help," and thanks to the people in Developmental Studies, I was able to achieve my goals.

Interviewer: What accommodations were made for your math disability?

Miss Barksley: For my math disability, the first accommodation that we needed was notetaking because without notes I could not take the test. The teacher devised a system called two-column notetaking and I had someone take the notes in class for me and after I noticed I was getting better notes with the system of two-column notetaking than the notetaker was, I was able to do it myself and that has helped me to go into my regular core algebra classes. I also still have a notetaker which enables me to pay more attention to the concepts that the teacher is explaining.

Interviewer: What do you believe to be your academic strengths?

Miss Barksley: My academic strength is my ability to write—so papers and my verbal communication is very, very efficient.

Interviewer: What strengths do you possess in your character and personality?

Miss Barksley: Good question. I think I have a positive attitude. That's my greatest asset. I realize that good things come to those who wait [persevere] and my ability to be patient. I realize that I have a problem and I realized I needed to confront it to achieve my goals. Therefore, I needed to persevere and to achieve it.

Interviewer: What things have you learned here at college that you feel will help you in the job you will get after graduating?

Miss Barksley: The most important thing is to learn to work with people and I understand that they have some problems of their own. No one is perfect and that if you learn to work with them, you can help them to work for themselves and to become more independent and advocates for themselves. If you don't know there is a problem then I can't help you and that is my objective in social work—to help others to know that they can overcome their obstacles themselves, not me overcome the obstacles for them.

Interviewer: If you had the opportunity to talk to administrators at college, what would you tell them?

Miss Barksley: The first thing I would say is to continue to hire faculty that is supportive of students, in tune with student's needs. I can remember being a senior in high school and wanting to do algebra and walking up to the teacher and she's telling me, "You can't do math." The next semester, I walked up to her with college application papers which said if you have a disability then you need to provide the proper documentation. She looked at me and said, "You want to go to college? You'll never make it." Well, fooled her. I did. Therefore, I think if faculty is in tune to student needs and can feel what the student is feeling and the student allows them to feel, then success for students will be possible. The second thing I would say is that support groups are very beneficial to students because they see other students achieving the goals that they have set for themselves and therefore it teaches them to be advocates for themselves, to achieve the goals that they want to achieve.

Clearly, Miss Barksley expresses the importance of interaction between herself and her teachers. The open student-faculty contact she experienced at college helped bridge the gaps she needed to be a successful college algebra student. Her positive attitude and verbal communication skills may have been more sharply focused and motivated by, oddly enough, her frustrating student-faculty contact with her high school mathematics teacher. She also implies strongly the importance of interaction in a united administrative organization to promote student success.

Miss Barksley was not initially a wheelchair user before college, but it was important to her educational goals to adapt to the wheelchair so that her physical demands were decreased. She was not academically prepared to enroll immediately in college algebra but it was important to her educational goals to strengthen her mathematics skills in order to go into college algebra and to learn appropriate techniques for seeking required help. Cooperation among the student with a disability, caring professors, and administrative units promoting academic networking for success helps make it possible for students like Angela Barksley to attain their immediate educational goals and to provide the framework for life-long learning.

Successful accommodations occur through ongoing dialogue between the student and the professor. It is imperative that the results of this dialogue be to communicate the common educational goals and to explore and develop together the manner in which these goals are to be achieved. It is the professor's responsibility to extend an invitation to all students to seek academic assistance from him. Thus the first questions that the professor must ask of himself are, "Do I have a statement in my syllabus that encourages any student to come to my office to discuss his/her learning needs?" and "Do I convey during class and during office hours that I can be approached for learning assistance?" It is imperative that this invitation be issued throughout the semester. Once the student initiates dialogue by asking for help, the professor who is a good teacher will naturally interact with various probing questions asked of himself and of the student.

The professor should ask the following questions of himself:
1. Do I need to discuss with the student and the Disability Support Services Office alternate formats of course materials?
2. Do I need to incorporate appropriate teaching adjustments during class time?
3. Do I verbalize accurately what is written on the board or overhead projector?
4. Would it be more effective to do certain in-class work at a different time and/or location? What is the best way to schedule this?
5. Do I seek out advice from other faculty who have had experience working with students who have the same or similar disability?
6. Do I maintain the standards for academic excellence by preserving the course content when I need to modify the presentation of materials?

The questions below should be asked by the professor of the student requesting assistance:
7. In what academic subjects have you experienced success?
8. Why do you believe you were successful?

9. What do you consider your strengths to be? What do you find difficult?
10. What specifically do you do to prepare for class? for a test?

At the postsecondary level, the professor is the subject matter expert. However, the student, also an experienced adult, is the expert on his particular mode of learning. The student with a disability has had to accomplish much for admittance to a college or university; thus, this student's insights are invaluable to the understanding of the professor who must make the necessary adaptations in the traditional classroom. The merging of subject matter expertise—the professor—and self-knowledge about learning—the student—is key to student success. Once the professor who is a good teacher understands the manner in which the student learns, adaptations evolve and accommodations naturally take place.

In the following subchapter note that despite the many things that make each learner different, there are "obvious" things that the professor can practice with every student. Again, consistent and ongoing interaction between student and faculty is an important first step to provide reasonable accommodations to students with disabilities; but more importantly it is an essential first step for maturity in the learning process by the student.

Don't Overlook the Obvious
by Maxine Elmont

Students with disabilities is a very diverse group who break down into many small populations, each of which has its own special needs. In our search for new techniques and methods to better help students to reach their potential, to enjoy success and accomplishment, we often overlook the obvious. For example, my first goal is to have students understand what I am all about, to either confirm or reject the stories that have preceded me. It is important to begin our relationship based on open, honest communication, which hopefully will translate into trust within a short period of time. First, all students need to know what is expected of them. Second, students should feel comfortable enough to speak without fear of retribution. This sounds easy, but, as we know, too many students bring with them a lack of trust for the authority figure. I have only fifteen weeks to try to reverse this attitude. I must be consistent in dealing with students. They have to know what to expect and being consistent is one way of reassuring them that what they see is what they get. Students with special needs have to be encouraged to discuss these with the instructor. Thus they are told to talk with me regarding any accommodations or services necessary to assist them in meeting the course objectives. Too often, individuals are reluctant to disclose their disability. They are more apt to deny that they may have a problem. If this is the case, I may not become aware of the disability until a few weeks into the course. While it is difficult to make up the lost time, I will approach the student and offer the necessary help.

The following are some of my experiences:

1. Andrew was a quadriplegic. His back was broken in an automobile accident. He was a young adult reentry student whose mobility depended upon his wheelchair and the assistance of other members of the college community. One of the first concerns was his inability to take notes. I asked the students who would be willing to share their notes with him. Since perception is selective, notes from more than one classmate allows a broader sense of what was presented and/or discussed. He provided the paper and carbon paper to the designated notetakers. This way he was given the notes at the end of each class. Andrew was a bright man, very articulate, actively participating in and contributing to all class discussions. The accommodations for test taking were mutually agreed upon. He was to take the exam in class with the other students. This meant he had access to me for questions, reassurance, and any other guidance that was given to the class as a whole. A volunteer scribe did all the writing. They sat slightly apart from the others so their communicating with each other would not be distracting or disturbing. While I was willing to extend the time, this was never a necessity. He did well in my class, his other courses, and transferred to and graduated from Boston University.

2. Mary was a recent high school graduate who regularly attended all sessions. She was quiet and interacted on a very limited basis during class. It was difficult to surmise if she would do well or merely "squeak by" her first multiple choice test. If students read, listen, and take notes in class, they should be able to pass the test unless there are special problems that have not been addressed. The test is set up to help them achieve. It is not an obstacle course where there are only a few winners. Mary's low score was a red flag to me. It was important to discover what was or was not happening. While discussing how she felt about the course, how she studied, and how she prepared for the exam, she told me that she was dyslexic but chose not to disclose this information. She did not want to ask for favors. When she realized that an accommodation was a right and not a favor, we were able to plan for the next test. She had the responsibility of seeing me regarding any material she needed clarified and we agreed that I would put the next test on tape. She would take it in class and use as much time as necessary. In addition to the exams, research was required of each student. While Mary's test scores improved, she found the amount of work overwhelming. She was carrying a full course load and working part-time. My task was to present as many alternatives to her as possible and remind her that education is to be enjoyable, not a bitter pill that she had to take. Her decision was to continue working, take a reduced course load, and finish her degree in five or six semesters rather than four. While she withdrew from my course, she was welcome to continue attending class since she was planning to repeat the course. Mary was not a strong student and this decision allowed her to survive academically. She also remained at work, from which she derived a great deal of pleasure and satisfaction.

3. Carl was a middle-aged male who said he needed an education if he were ever to become financially independent. His behavior indicated that he had some serious emotional problems. He had a very low frustration threshold and became

extremely agitated if he felt things were not going the way he wanted. Carl would become verbally aggressive in the hope of intimidating or coercing people into getting his way. Unfortunately, he wasn't at the point where he was ready to be part of a group. His demands and lack of patience were not compatible with class goals that require cooperation and the setting aside of tremendous personal needs. The system had failed him early in life, when he was diagnosed and treated as retarded rather than a very bright individual who had emotional problems. As an adult, however, he has learned—or believes he has learned—to make the system work for him. He would go from office to office in search of anyone who would tell him what he wanted to hear. Carl was not a danger to anyone, but the demands he made on professional and support staff were unreasonable and inappropriate. As his advisor, the dean decided I would be the one to deal with his requests. This was acceptable to him but it was extremely time consuming. He needed constant reassurance and limit setting. Needless to say he did not always respond to limit setting in a positive way. Carl wanted to be in school but he sabotaged virtually every chance of success. It was easier for him to deal with failure because it had become a familiar pattern. After meeting with several of my colleagues, we felt the word processing certificate program might be the answer for him rather than the liberal arts major he had chosen. Carl and I discussed the pros and cons of this option. Carl met with the word processing faculty and found them to be patient and supportive. He transferred to the program and at the end of the year, Carl not only graduated but also had a job waiting for him. Commencement was an achievement for him and an accomplishment for those of us who had worked so long and hard with him. Seeing him wear his cap and gown with pride and dignity gave a new meaning to "a job well done."

Experience has taught me that students with disabilities should be treated as much like their nondisabled peers as possible. Whatever accommodations have to be made should be done with minimal confusion and fanfare. Perhaps the basic key to working with persons who are disabled is time, patience, and the comfort or discomfort level of the instructor. There is no place for pity. Empathy not sympathy is necessary if these students are to achieve in academe and succeed in the world of work.

Providing "reasonable accommodations" for students with disabilities can be difficult because accommodations do not follow a given prescription for success. Qualified students with disabilities are not automatically entitled to receiving accommodations; they are, however, entitled to participate in a class in a manner that strives to eliminate the impact posed by the given disability. As more students with disabilities achieve educational and career goals and as legal proceedings continue to clarify how students are provided equal access to higher education, colleges and universities will increase expectations of faculty to provide appropriate teaching adjustments and accommodations that equalize learning for students impacted by various disabilities.

The first thing colleges and universities do to proclaim their expectations for faculty is to issue a brochure or handbook to them. The purpose of this brochure is to impart knowledge about the issues of disabilities that may be lacking in the professor's educational training and to provide awareness of those parts of the united administrative organization responsible for supporting the interaction necessary between faculty and students with disabilities. The focus of this brochure is "to heighten awareness and provide basic information for the benefit of both faculty and students" (Lissner, 1992). An excellent example of such a brochure is *A Guide to Reasonable Accommodations for Students with Disabilities*. It was written by L. Scott Lissner and is used at Longwood College, Farmville, Virginia.

The following chapters present anecdotal subchapters illustrating instructional accommodations that have proven successful by professors in higher education. The chapters represent eight functional impact categories: (1) attention, concentration, or memory difficulties; (2) chronic health problems; (3) hearing impairments or deafness; (4) integrative processing difficulties; (5) mobility impairments or motor control difficulties; (6) social behavior disorders or difficulties with consistent performance; (7) speech and language difficulties; and (8) visual impairments and blindness. Beside each subchapter are margin notes that emphasize key points in the accommodation and learning process. To begin each chapter, the impact area is defined and accompanied by a list of commonly associated disabilities. Since students may have multiple disabilities or one disability may have multiple impacts, the lists are not prescriptive, but are rather a starting point for the professor to establish communication links with the student and to begin the investigation of meaningful teaching and learning strategies for the student. To conclude each impact area, a list of frequently used instructional accommodations is given.

REFERENCES

Chickering, A. W. & Gamson, Z. F. (1987). "Seven Principles for Good Practice in Undergraduate Education," [Special section]. *The Wingspread Journal*, 9(2).

Heath Resource Center. (1988). *The Head Injury Survivor on Campus: Issues and Resources*. [Brochure]. Washington, DC.

Heath Resource Center. (1987). *Learning Disabled Adults in Postsecondary Education*. [Brochure]. Washington, DC.

Heath Resource Center. (1990). *Students Who are Deaf or Hard of Hearing in Postsecondary Education*. [Brochure]. Washington, DC.

Heath Resource Center. (1992). *Students Who are Blind or Visually Impaired in Postsecondary Education*. [Brochure]. Washington, DC.

Hodge, B. M. & Preston-Sabin, J. E. (1994). "An interview with Angela Barksley." *The Challenges and Rewards of Teaching Students with Disabilities*. Unpublished manuscript, Austin Peay State University, Clarksville, TN.

Lissner, L. S. (1992). *A Guide to Reasonable Accommodations for Students with Disabilities* (interim ed.) [Brochure]. Longwood College, Farmville, VA.

Chapter 4
TEACHING STUDENTS WITH ATTENTION, CONCENTRATION, OR MEMORY DIFFICULTIES

A student with attention, concentration, or memory difficulties may experience problems in one or more of the following areas: following a lecture, timed reading, spelling, and short-term memorizing. The student may also appear to daydream or fall asleep in class. The disability is often not visible. (Lissner, 1992)

Commonly Associated Disabilities

attention deficit disorder
psychological disorders
learning disabilities
clinical depression
seizure disorders
head trauma
narcolepsy
tinnitus
agnosia
aphasia

The establishment of good communication is the foundation of student success. Here is a list of questions to consider or discuss with the student who has difficulties in attention, concentration, or memory.

1. In what way can I help this student to focus on my lecture with a minimum of disruption or embarrassment in the classroom?
2. Which mode of communication has provided the most success in the student's previous courses—reading, writing, speaking, or listening?
3. Has the student ever used a tape recorder to tape classes? How has it worked?
4. Has the student utilized notecards as study aids? If so, specifically how?
5. Would the student benefit by using a notetaker in class?
6. What aids, besides the textbook, would be helpful to the student?

Identifying Good Teaching Practices
by Charles Babb

"I couldn't afford to learn it," said the Mock Turtle with a sigh. "I only took the regular course."

"What was that?" enquired Alice.

"Reeling and Writhing, of course, to begin with," the Mock Turtle replied; "and then the different branches of Arithmetic—Ambition, Distraction, Uglification, and Derision." (*The Annotated Alice*, Lewis Carroll, notes by Martin Gardner, New York: Bramhall House, 1960, p. 129)

Good communication is necessary in replacing assumptions with facts.

While trying to avoid generalities and altruisms, it must be said that the first and most important strategy in dealing with students in the classroom remains to never assume anything. What you write may not be what they see. What you say may not be what they hear. How you approach a problem may have no relationship to their perceptions of solving the same problem. The opening quotation does contain several atrocious puns, but it demonstrates my point. Also, it might very well describe the student's previous experiences in mathematics.

Discuss previous experiences in a similar course.

There is no way of describing the "typical" disabled student. A specific example, however, can shed light on what strategies might be employed. Karen came into my math skills classroom diagnosed as dyslexic. Her athletic advisor made sure that all her instructors were aware of Karen's disability before the school year began. The following are the strategies that I employed while Karen was in my math skills classroom.

A campus support network is helpful.

Acknowledge differences in learning styles in methods of presentation in the classroom.

1. I would say out loud everything that I wrote on the board or on overhead transparencies.

This was especially true at the beginning of a unit. For example, $3(x + 2)^2$, may have a great deal of meaning for me in an early algebra unit, but Karen was better served by hearing, "Three times left parenthesis x plus 2 right parenthesis with exponent two" than by anything that I could write. Then I would remind her of where and how an exponent is written and what an exponent means. Later on, this was read, "Three left paren x plus two right paren to the second power."

2. I established an atmosphere of tolerance and, when possible, had Karen explain what she was doing, step-by-step, as she proceeded through a problem.

I can learn a lot about a student's reasoning skills by listening. If Karen couldn't explain what she was doing, then as I watched I would ask questions similar to the following:

Establish an atmosphere of tolerance and openness.

Why line up the decimal points when adding decimals?

What does adding the same number to both sides of an equation do to the equation? Do you have to do it that way?

What is the number under the division symbol called and why would I want to know that?

Carefully listen to responses for clues to learning.

Is there a skill from arithmetic that explains this step in algebra?

3. I presented new material in as many formats as possible.
For each topic that I taught I created or found as many of the following as Karen could handle: handouts, overheads, videos, worksheets, audio cassettes. Each student in any classroom may have a different learning style. This seems to be especially true of students with disabilities like Karen's.

Address the diversity of student learning styles.

4. I always tried to remember that it was ultimately up to Karen to learn, and up to me to make learning possible.
I may not be aware that a student has a learning disability; but if I use preemptive strategies and involve the student early on in learning activities, then I have a chance of discovering possible problems. As the instructor I must be a leader. To lead, there must be willing followers. Many disabled students come to me with a great deal of emotional baggage due to past failures. Karen had other successes to make up for academic failures. I realize that every student is an individual and try to figure out what the best strategy is for that person.

Both the instructor and the student have clear roles in the learning process.

The preceding list of strategies can be employed in every class session regardless of the types of disabilities present. I taught Karen for three semesters. She successfully progressed through beginning algebra and finally through a combined intermediate and college algebra course. She graduated on time with an overall grade point average of 3.25 and lettered in three sports. While I was specifically dealing with her disability, other students in my classes benefited from the teaching strategies I was employing.

Other students benefit from diversity in teaching—not just the student with a disability.

Frank: Advocating for Oneself
by Susan Bartzak-Graham

Like many other part-time faculty, I frequently find students in learning situations that are complicated by the part-time nature of my commitment to the class I am teaching. Even in an institution with reasonable and accessible academic support services, there are some students who elect not to utilize services and depend upon you, as a faculty member, to serve as the sole mediator between you and the material. Frank began as such a student.

The connection between students and professors is critical when other support services are not readily available.

I met Frank at a local community college during the first session of an 8:00 A.M. Introduction to Psychology class. The class met on Tuesdays and Thursdays until 9:15 A.M., and I needed to be able to report to my full-time administrative position, a minimum of one half-hour away by car on a good day, no later than 10:00 A.M.

Frank was a member of a thirty-five-student class, approximately two-thirds male, most between the ages of 19 and 22. Several came directly to school from work. As in most community colleges, their rationale for choosing this course, in particular, and for being in school, in general, was diverse.

Frank sat in the second row of a four-row lecture classroom, close to the left-hand side of the room, with a Metallica-tee-shirted friend from his recently ended high school days. Initially, he seemed no more or less attentive or perplexed than other students in the class, but I did recognize that he did not record a great volume of notes.

At the end of the third week of class, right before our first quiz, Frank shared with me the fact that he had several learning disabilities, and had been involved in Chapter 766 programs for most of his academic life. What then followed was an adversarial game of cat and mouse about accommodations that could be made for him, a technique that I have found to be not uncommon among students with extensive exposure to the label of "learning disabled." I would ask him what he needed; he would ask me what I could do. I would ask him what had worked for him in high school; he would ask me to tell him what I had found to work with students I had taught previously. He was unable to put a name on his disabilities, so I suggested "routine" accommodations like untimed testing, and recording lectures; he agreed that these accommodations were appropriate, but wanted to know if there was anything else that I could do. I finally told him that until I knew what his disabilities were, it would be difficult to determine what further accommodations I could, or needed, to make. He also mentioned that while

Documentation must exist and must be on file.

A Disability Support Services Office is necessary to provide consistency and fairness.

he sought these accommodations, he did not want to stand out from the rest of the class.

Before the next class session, Frank brought in a learning profile sheet from Academic Support Services, which detailed his *Development of* learning strengths and weaknesses, and made recommendations for *a learning* instructional accommodations. At the end of class, we sat down *profile is* *important.* and discussed what we could do together to make the class a positive learning experience for him. We agreed that he would bring his laptop to class to assist him in taking notes, as his typing was faster than his longhand writing. I agreed to outline each lecture prior to the class, and to give him a photostat of my notes, *Outline of* so that he could fill gaps. We agreed to have either untimed or *lectures was* take-home tests during the semester, which would allow him the *provided.* additional time he needed without making his need for untimed testing an issue for the rest of the class. Because another class *Accommodation* started fifteen minutes after ours ended, and I had no office to use, *should be made* we decided that in-class tests would begin at 7:30 A.M., and that *available to all* we would make that start time available to anyone in the class who *students.* chose to use it.

I decided that students, on the final two exams, would have the option of taking a free response (essay) or multiple choice/true- *Students are* false exam. I believed that, in this way, Frank could view both *allowed choice* tests, and decide which one would enable him to put forth his best *in testing* *formats.* effort. The opportunity to choose the mode of expression would also not place any stigma on him individually because all students would have the same option.

We also talked about the issue of self-advocacy; how Frank might move from asking what could be offered, to letting his *Self-advocacy is* instructors know what he needed in order to have his learning *important.* needs met. As the semester went on, we extended the discussion to family issues, which he believed impeded his learning, and by the end of the semester, I believe that he became more assertive about *There is a need* his need for family support. *for early*

Frank was only the first of many students with learning disabil- *invitation and* *ongoing* ities who shared information about their learning histories with me *dialogue for* that semester. A few students shared their stories too late in the *student success.* semester for me to take the kind of steps that I believe would have been necessary for them to succeed to their potential in the class. The accommodations that were originally made for Frank *The ultimate* enhanced the performance of a number of class members. *goal is for* *students to* However, I wish that I could have done more for the young man *reach their* who knew the material, and could relate it with comic brilliance to *learning* his personal life, but was unable to develop further con- *potential.* ceptualizations. His final paper and presentation entitled, "Everything You Always Wanted to Know about the Brain, but Were Afraid to Ask," eloquently addressed how it feels to be considered "different" and "stupid" by a system that does not often recognize more than one or two of Gardner's seven intelligences.

Back to Frank—he passed the course, with a hard-fought B-, a realistic grade in terms of his understanding of the material, and his ability to apply it to further learning, and to his life. But I hope that he came away from the course with more than an understanding of how the theories of Freud, Erickson, Skinner, and others operate. I hope that he came away from the course with an increased sense of his ability to do academic coursework, and an appreciation for himself as one who chooses to advocate for himself as a learner.

As faculty, and especially part-time faculty, it is difficult to reach every student we teach, and to attempt to give them a sense of self-worth as a learner that systems often deny them. Yet, using Frank as an example, if we are willing to make small accommodations, we can empower students to take more control of their own learning and of its outcomes in academic and nonacademic areas of their lives.

Textbook Marking: An Aid to Concentration, Comprehension, and Retention
by Verdery B. Kennedy

Sara sat on the back row of my third-quarter developmental reading class. She looked angry, defiant and thoroughly miserable. She glared at me throughout that first class session—an open invitation for someone to *do something* about her plight. I normally don't conference with students until after their first test, allowing me time to get a feel for their abilities, but this case clearly called for immediate action. Sara looked ready to explode.

A long conversation in my office resulted in tears of frustration and relief rather than an explosion. Sara confessed that she *hated* to read and that she found college to be even more frustrating than high school, where her active involvement in sports had broken up the tedium of study. She had had little trouble learning to read, especially enjoying the games, skits, and drawing projects inherent in the early elementary learning process. She had had no problem reading the short assignments, especially if she used a piece of paper or her finger to guide her eyes along a line of print. Her dislike of reading began in middle school where reading assignments became longer. She hated to sit for long periods of time and generally broke reading sessions up by frequent forays to the kitchen or play time outside. At this point she was encouraged and then forced to abandon the crutch of focusing her attention with a pointing finger. By the time she reached high school, she was having trouble concentrating in the classroom as well as on reading assignments, since most classes required her to sit at a desk throughout the entire period. Her grades were not strong in classes requiring a lot of reading, but she got by through copying her classmates' notes and memorizing the material as she paced up and down in her room. Even though her verbal SAT was low, she did well enough to enter college provisionally.

In all three areas of developmental studies her first quarter, she exited math easily as well as composition, because her papers were based on personal experience rather than on reading assignments. She did especially well on papers she wrote outside of class because she could think on her feet, sitting down only to do the actual writing. In fact, she did so much better on these outside papers that at one point her instructor had questioned her honesty. She was now in her third quarter of developmental reading and struggling with an English course requiring analysis papers on literature. She had passed her mathematics class with a B and failed history and psychology with an F and D, respectively. She had come nowhere near making a passing score on the reading exit exam—a timed, standardized test. Sara was convinced that she was intelligent, but feared something was wrong with her because she could neither concentrate on her reading assignments nor remember much of what she read.

My conversation with Sara revealed that she was both articulate and intelligent. Discrete questioning revealed that she had never been diagnosed or even tested for learning disabilities, but she had been in remedial reading classes in middle school. My first response was to refer her to the testing center for LD screening. The waiting list is long, however.

With Sara in her third quarter of developmental studies, I couldn't wait for the results of the tests, so I administered an informal learning styles inventory I'd picked up at a conference the previous spring. As I expected, Sara's scores showed her to be a strong kinesthetic/tactile learner, with both visual and auditory being minor styles. Sara's troubles with concentration, comprehension and retention were likely caused by her failure to utilize learning strategies that supported her major learning style.

Students have a preferred learning style, but are often unaware of what it is or how to use it to maximize their learning opportunities.

Having recently reread Mortimer Adler's classic article, "How to Mark a Book," in addition to exploring several articles on learning styles and studying reading and study skills texts that advocated strategies supporting multiple learning styles, I began to teach Sara kinesthetic strategies that would enhance her concentration, comprehension, and memory. The first step was to give her back her "crutch." This time it took the form of a pen or pencil instead of her finger or a piece of paper. She resisted this approach at first because she had been thoroughly schooled in the idea that the "crutch" was both infantile and wrong. Getting used to using her crutch again took only a few days, however. Sara quickly discovered that when she used it her need for physical activity during reading was at least partially satisfied, reducing her fidgeting and resulting in a marked increase in concentration. She also discovered that she could control her reading rate, speeding up or slowing down depending on the difficulty of the material, which resulted in an overall increase in reading speed.

The next step was to teach Sara an efficient method of marking her text, which would further increase her concentration through active mental as well as physical involvement in the reading

Students should be actively involved in their learning.

process. Until they enter college, most students have attended schools where marking in their textbooks is strictly forbidden, and Sara's experience had been no exception to this rule. This is unfortunate because research has shown that text marking is the single most effective strategy for both comprehension and retention. For kinesthetic/tactile learners it may even be essential for learning, and since many learning disabled students are kinesthetic/tactile, text marking should be taught to them as a matter of course. Sara

The use of textbook marking is effective for many kinesthetic learners.

quickly learned that marking her text benefited her in the following ways:

1. It focused her attention on the task at hand and became an invaluable aid to concentration.
2. It enhanced her comprehension by keeping her actively involved in the reading process through making decisions and organizing. She had to decide what and how to mark in order to organize the material for easy recognition of major and minor points and their relationships to each other.
3. It provided instant feedback, for if she could not decide how to mark, she knew immediately that she did not understand the material and needed to reread or get help.
4. It gave her a skeleton outline of the information to be studied, thus cutting down on the amount of time needed for review. In the past, Sara had attempted to reread her text and notes until she had memorized them. This impossibly time-consuming task had resulted in only minimal retention. Marking her text, on the other hand, allowed her to spend study and review time on the essentials of the course.

The marking process I taught Sara included the following:

Highlight the topic or subject of each section or paragraph of the main idea when given. She also highlighted or boxed important terms. These represent the concepts of the course and figure prominently in test questions.

Underline major supporting details. These would be test answers.

Circle transitional or signal words—as a result, for example, on the other hand.

Label definitions, examples, potential test questions, and material she did not understand.

Number listed items. If the author signaled items in a sequence with first, second, last, etc., she could simply circle these signal words. Often, however, these signals are not present, so she needed to add small circled numbers. After items were numbered, she was to add the number to the heading or write a heading in the margin, for example, "(6) Causes of Bubonic Plague."

I encouraged Sara to ask questions to guide her reading and marking as per the SQ3R system (developed by Frances P. Robinson) and to read each paragraph or section *before* marking. Those who mark as they read tend to mark too much. I encouraged her to develop her own symbols and to be consistent with her marking from course to course. She discovered that once she had developed a workable system she could use it with only minor modifications with everything she read. After she finished an assignment, she was to check her marking to be sure that all key points stood out clearly.

My goal was for Sara to be able to see at a glance (1) the distinction between main points and supporting details; (2) the nature or category of the support: comparison/contrast, example, definition, cause/effect, etc.; and (3) the relationship between ideas.

Have clear goals in mind when suggesting and implementing strategies to students.

Sara worked all quarter to perfect her new skills and found that by applying them, she could for the first time in her school career concentrate for extended periods of reading, comprehend what she was reading, and to her great delight, remember what she had read. She was able to pass the standardized exit exam due to her developed ability to concentrate on a reading task for a full hour and her increased reading speed. She passed her third quarter of developmental reading with an A, her English class with a C, and the history course she was retaking with a B. The results of Sara's LD screening came near the end of the quarter and revealed that she had a very mild attention deficit disorder that could be controlled by using kinesthetic/tactile strategies both in the class-room and while reading. In June of 1991, Sara graduated from Georgia Southern with a degree in Early Childhood Education and intends to focus her teaching on the individual learning styles of her students and encourage all of her kinesthetic/tactile students to use "the crutch." I learned a great deal from my experience with Sara and now teach all of my students study techniques that support their individual learning styles.

Katrina: Test Anxiety and User-Friendly Surroundings
by Sari Rosenheck

Katrina was an adult student in my writing class. She was a single mom, educationally disadvantaged, probably learning disabled, and extremely nervous in testing situations.

Katrina appeared to be a dedicated student. She asked for extra help from me, went for tutoring religiously, and claimed that she put in hours of study time. What her homework, papers, and grades said was an entirely different story.

One clue that there may be a hidden disability is when test scores and "in-class" assignments do not match those done outside of class.

Katrina's papers were a disaster; her thoughts were so disorganized I could barely follow them, and grammar and punctuation were nonexistent. What finally made the difference for both of us was a weekly quiz.

Every Wednesday I give my class the same type of quiz. It consists of ten vocabulary words and a quotation that they have to comment on in two paragraphs. Every Wednesday Katrina would leave the class close to tears, lamenting on the fact that she studied for hours for the vocabulary and, as for the quotes, would say "it never comes out on paper the way it starts in my head!"

After one particular quiz, with an extremely distraught Katrina, I suggested we try something different. I had her come with me back to the Tutoring Center and immediately took her to a study room. I told her that since she felt she had already failed the quiz, she had nothing to lose. Then I asked her to simply tell me the definitions of the words, calmly, without pressure. We did the same with her essay; I had her "talk" her essay, instead of writing it for me under testing circumstances.

No, she did not immediately give the correct responses orally, but what she was able to do was hear her own voice. She was then apparently able to correct herself; because I let her "talk it out" and withheld my initial response, she would ultimately come up with the correct answer.

I have to smile to myself. Mine is a writing class, and on occasion I do test my students orally. Once or twice is really all that is needed for students to grasp correct responses to questions. This seems to work well with English as a Second Language (ESL) students, also. After the first time testing a student orally, a smile and the comment "just like last time, remember?" relaxes them, and reminds them of a recent academic success.

Katrina knew she had test anxiety. What she didn't know was that it could be managed. Just living through the worst case scenario (failing the quizzes) and showing her that she would survive helped. She also attended workshops on test anxiety and study skills given by the Center for Learning Assistance.

This little exercise with Katrina wasn't earth-shattering; it didn't change her life in a lot of big ways. What it did was show Katrina that all of her studying was not in vain. She was certainly capable of learning. It also showed her that given user-friendly surroundings, she was able to call up the information she needed. *Accentuate the positive—all students are capable of learning.*

More than anything else Katrina was shown the most important lesson we learn as educators, that different people may study, test, and ultimately learn in different ways, and that is O.K.!

Math Strategies for Linda
by Karyn L. Schulz

Linda contacted me through the Office of Special Services. Her counselor, the Learning Disabilities Specialist, said she needed math tutoring for developmental arithmetic. Prior to our first session, I read her documentation and learned some important information about her. We obtained documentation from the student's high school on a recent psychoeducational test. We cannot provide support services without this documentation. I learned that her disability had been diagnosed as learning disabled with Attention Deficit Disorder. She had taken special education classes since elementary school. Her documentation also reported a well-mannered, eager-to-please student. I looked forward to working with her. *Long-term documentation of the student's learning history can provide insight about how the student learns.*

Linda was placed into developmental arithmetic because of her placement tests taken upon registering for classes at Essex Community College. The placement test is campus designed and geared to determine the correct level math course that a student should register for first, to assure success. Linda scored low on her placement tests and she was placed directly into developmental arithmetic in a special lecture setting. Her disability had been identified in auditory discrimination/listening, reading, writing, and mathematics. In addition, the student had a history of emotional and possibly psychiatric problems and a doctor also noted that she displayed hyperactivity.

Communication with student input is essential to planning educational goals.

I set up an appointment with Linda to discuss what she felt her needs would be and what tutoring I could provide. She said that she needed tutoring in developmental arithmetic and developmental reading. During the initial session, we reviewed her notetaking skills, study habits, and test-taking skills. After much conversation about her previous accomplishments and mistakes, we agreed that the three skills mentioned needed much improvement.

Linda came to me needing strategies to be successful in her classes. She was very eager to use these strategies, but felt that she had barriers to overcome. These included poor self-esteem and her instructors' openness to make teaching adaptations. She had poor study habits when she entered college, which was the same in high school.

Ongoing meetings establish individualized adaptations for the student.

I asked her to demonstrate her study techniques for arithmetic. She proceeded to open the textbook and read, and read, and read. This obviously was not working and not appropriate for arithmetic. We then brainstormed ideas for studying arithmetic, which was difficult for the student. Linda was having a very difficult time with fractions. She could not follow the required procedures necessary to manipulate fractions. I suggested the following:

1. Tape record the steps for making equivalent fractions and then listen to the steps when she has difficulties completing a problem.
2. Make a study sheet using examples of problems to follow. For ex-

   ample, $\frac{a}{c} \times \frac{b}{d} = \frac{ab}{cd}$. She would then plug numbers into this so

   that it matched the ones she had done.
3. The most obvious study habit that I encouraged was to practice, practice, practice. This made sense to her when she realized that a-rithmetic is application.
4. Use index cards that have a different rule of arithmetic on the front and an example of that rule on the back. I encouraged her to obtain 4 x 6 cards for more space. Her support system at home was strong and she said that someone could quiz her on the flashcards.

Learning how to learn helps the student learn content.

Linda began using these techniques and reported some progress, but not necessarily in fractions. She did feel more confident in herself with her study habits and that she was giving herself an advantage by repeated practice. She said that this made her more aware of her errors and also her successes.

Testing in arithmetic was also a concern of Linda's. She felt intimidated by the exams because of the amount of material written on one side of the paper. The amount of material facing her at once was overwhelming and stressful. I discussed this with the instructor who was also willing to make some changes. I suggested rewriting her tests by "blocking" her problems so the student can focus better on each question. The instructor liked this idea and made the necessary changes but Linda still had difficulty with her exams. Even with the tests now being blocked by the instructor, Linda still felt overwhelmed by the amount of questions on the paper. I suggested further blocking while she was testing by placing pieces of blank paper over the other questions while she was focusing on the problem she was working on. This kept her distractions limited and her attention on target and it proved to be a very successful test-taking tool for her. She began to use this technique for other exams as well.

We continued to work on arithmetic during the semester and then began to work on developmental reading. Many of the same techniques used in arithmetic worked here. We designed flashcards for vocabulary, grammar, and punctuation rules. Linda felt that the flashcards helped improve many of her skills. I explained that they improved her memory skills by repeated practice of the material while also being a multisensory self-teaching tool. She would be using vision, hearing by reading aloud as she wrote, and tactile senses by touching the pencil and the index card. She also used blocking techniques here during her testing. The reading tests were standardized and could not be rewritten in a less stimulating format. She learned to use the blank papers for covering the preceding and the following questions so she could focus and not feel overwhelmed by the exam. Her reading skills improved over the course of the semester and she finished the course with a satisfactory grade.

Compensating strategies can be used in different academic settings and leads to lifetime learning.

Linda passed both courses. She registered for developmental algebra the following semester, which was a big ego boost. She had never gotten beyond the arithmetic level before in school, and felt quite proud of herself. She had made numerous friends in the office area and all knew of her accomplishment. She did not, however, return to Essex a year later. She felt she needed to mature and do some self-exploration by working in the real world. She has kept in touch with me and realizes that her decision was a wise one.

My experience with Linda was rewarding. Her eagerness to succeed was tremendous. Her growth, both academically and emotionally, was also rewarding. Together we learned, laughed, and cried.

The Many Uses of Cassette Tapes in Teaching Composition to Learning Disabled Students
by Nancy A. Stricklin

Use different methods for assessing the same type of assignment.

After having taught English at a two-year college for a year, I quickly realized that traditional methods of teaching and grading for principally nontraditional students were not as effective as I would have liked. In particular, I was always baffled by how to help students who worked full-time and who were thus marginal in their attendance and often unable to attend individual conferences. In an attempt to rectify this problem, I began to rely heavily on cassette tapes as a means of providing students with access to the lectures they missed and oral responses to their papers.

At the beginning of the semester, I purchased a number of tapes for my own use and then asked each student to purchase a cassette tape, which was to be handed to me along with certain designated compositions. I then explained to the students that I intended to tape my classes so that they could listen to the tapes should they be absent and that I intended to use their tapes as a grading tool. I planned to alternate three modes for grading their compositions: the holistic method, the standard method (a weighted grade and written comments), and the taped method (written and oral comments).

As the semester progressed, the reaction to the taped method was overwhelmingly supportive, and in adopting it, I was able also to discern other applications for its usage, particularly with students diagnosed as learning disabled. Eventually, I began to use the tapes not only for taping my lectures and for grading compositions, but also for assigning specific oral exercises to students who were having difficulties with certain aspects of composition primarily due to their disabilities.

During the summer in which I adopted the method, a student came to me at the end of the first class meeting and told me that she had been diagnosed in high school with Attention Deficit Disorder (ADD) and that she would appreciate any additional help and consideration I might offer her. From my cursory reading about students with ADD, I realized that focusing upon the lectures for fifty minutes would prove difficult for her. I also realized that she might require more than the traditional approach to the course—lecture, individualized instruction, and peer interaction. In discussing her disability with her, I began to realize that the tapes might prove helpful in more ways than I had originally anticipated, and I was correct. Eventually the tapes, coupled with her own skill and determination, allowed her to make tremendous progress with her writing.

Students must recognize that they have skills; instructors must help them to identify and utilize these skills.

She found the tapes invaluable because they allowed her to listen to class lectures at her own pace and as often as she needed and they allowed her another method of understanding her problems with composition other than my written responses. In particular, they helped her to understand and virtually to eliminate one particular writing problem—the comma splice.

By and large, this student was a capable writer who had few grammatical or mechanical problems in her compositions, but her compositions were always riddled with comma splices. My written assessment of the problem and her own study of our grammar manual proved fruitless in addressing the problem; however, when she and I read her papers aloud during class immediately before she handed her papers in to be graded or afterward, during the revision process, she had more success in spotting her comma splices and correcting them. But, if she were left completely on her own to proofread or to revise, she often would have as many as three comma splices a page.

Thus, it soon became obvious to us both that she needed to *hear* her composition read aloud so that she could determine where one complete thought ended and another began. At this point, we decided it might be worth her while to read her composition into the tape recorder and then to play it back, so that she could hear where she herself seemed to end one sentence and to begin another. Obviously, this was a time-consuming method, and if she had not been determined to improve her writing, I doubt that the method would have been nearly as successful. On the basis of this method and her own effort, however, her final drafts soon evidenced little problem with the comma splice.

Students must be determined to succeed in order to translate that determination into actuality.

Because the method required so much time, I often gave her an extra day for her writing assignments. The result was well worth it for us both. By the end of the semester, she had reduced her comma splices from three to a page to only one or two for the entire composition.

Her own evaluation of the method speaks volumes: "It is difficult for me to imagine trying to improve my writing without the tapes. For problems with style, sentence variety, descriptive words and phrases, and the comma splice, the tape was very instructive."

Instructional Accommodations for Students
Impacted by Attention, Concentration, or Memory Difficulties

outlines provided for lectures
alternate location for testing
use of a scribe or notetaker
extended time for tests
series of short tests
tape record lectures
seating location
calculators

Chapter 5
TEACHING STUDENTS WITH CHRONIC HEALTH PROBLEMS

A student experiencing chronic health problems may have difficulties with general health from day to day or with endurance. This may affect the student's mobility, concentration, attendance, or physical exertion. (Lissner, 1992)

Commonly Associated Disabilities

cardiovascular disorders
muscular dystrophy
clinical depression
cystic fibrosis
cerebral palsy
head trauma
diabetes
AIDS

The establishment of good communication is the foundation of student success. Here is a list of questions to consider or discuss with the student who experiences a chronic health problem.

1. Is it possible that the student will have to miss class? If so, what arrangements will need to be made?
2. Has the student ever utilized time-management techniques such as daily, weekly, and monthly calendars?
3. What specifically are the physical limitations that impact the student's learning?
4. Would a notetaker in class be helpful?
5. What aids, besides the textbook, are most helpful to the student?
6. Has the student ever used a tape recorder to tape class notes?

Acceptance of Frustration—A Key to Learning
by Mary Brown

Acceptance of frustration seems to be a key to learning. In the sciences, persistence and time on task usually is crucial to success. My student population has been identified as students who have a deficient background in the sciences or who are science reluctant. Their goals are diverse and include a range of need, from seeking a professional career in a science-related field to passing the college's science requirement for graduation. The acceptance of frustration and the patience to devote the time necessary to assimilate information for themselves vary.

Sarah could be described as a typical student in my course, although an "atypical" student by other student measures. She is approximately forty-five years of age. She is returning to school after a fifteen-year employment record with a construction company. An injury on the job forced her to choose a less physical occupation. She is currently undecided about her future career but knows she must "use her mind more" than she has in the past fifteen years.

Sarah added the course late. She added the course based on a counselor's recommendation because she had "no background or knowledge in the sciences. I haven't had to use my brain for fifteen years and I'm not sure I'll remember how to!"

In a recent class discussion on science anxiety Sarah readily admitted that science scares her. She said she is afraid of not doing well in the course. She told her mostly younger classmates that it is very important for her to do well and that she takes this class seriously but that it is very difficult for her.

In the same class period the topic of coping with frustration when you are not doing well came up. Sarah volunteered that it is very important to stay with the topic even if you don't feel comfortable. She suggested that asking for help is an important skill although under used!

Sarah walked out of the first exam very frustrated. She told me it is important for her "not to give up." She felt she did a poor job showing her skills on the first exam and felt that she was actually doing better than the exam score indicates.

We use an instrument that analyzes student attitudes. The results indicate that learning has a component of disequilibrium within it. I pair conversion problems from English to metrics with a discussion of attitude shift. The problems are given as a homework assignment. At the next class period, I hear many complaints about the assignment. When the usual moans and groans about the level of difficulty come out, we talk about the attitude shift.

All students experience frustration when learning. It is not necessarily an indication of a disability, but rather "normal" progression through the learning process.

I point out to them that their level of frustration is a healthy part of the learning process. I also warn them not to get stuck in the complaining mode. The shift indicates it is important to move through that stage in order to achieve the "insight" phase. I cite experiences of past students who I have seen move through all stages, and revel in the joy of insight.

The change of their attitude is refreshing. It's almost as if you gave them permission to complain. They also recognize the signs of discouragement in classmates and try to help them through their difficulty. They recognize that complaints do not help them proceed toward their goal and that they must take more active steps. I believe understanding the attitude shift gives students more control over their own learning. They view the frustration experience as a positive sign, as an intermediate step toward insight.

Sarah stayed with the metric system. She also stayed within the course. During the semester, she had many situations of frustration. She found our unit on spatial perception very challenging. Indeed, on the day of the final review, Sarah was still struggling over the topographic maps. She was determined that she was not going to let that portion of the exam defeat her. Sarah earned a 3.5 on a 4-point scale for the course!

A colleague recently gave me a copy of an illustration depicting how a student's attitude will shift. It shows a top view of a house with four rooms. You enter into a room labeled contentment. This is the stage where you are not frustrated by challenges. The door to this room swings into denial. You are beginning the frustrating task and are in denial of your own difficulties with the task. The door to this room leads into confusion. As the task becomes more frustrating, you become confused. You have difficulty stepping back and looking at the task objectively. At this point, students often quit. But, if they quit they can't enter the next room, which is renewal. This is analogous to the insight experienced by students.

Next semester, I plan on pairing both the instrument with the poster illustration of the "learning rooms." I'm hoping that the added visual impact of the poster will help give students a good visual memory of the attitude shift. It should help increase persistence and time on tasks which are crucial to success in the sciences.

REFERENCES

Woods, Donald R. (1987). "Self-directed Learning, Creating Internal Representations, More Life Skills Materials." *Journal of College Science Teaching*, XV(4), 384–389.

Samantha: Time Management and Study Skills
by Eleanor Syler

Samantha was diagnosed with epilepsy at four years old. Throughout her life, she has undergone extensive testing and medical treatment and was placed in learning disability (LD) classes throughout her academic career. She reported having great difficulty learning and had to have tutors during the summer to help her keep up with her class. During the eighth and ninth grades she attended a small private school that offered independent study, yet she still had to have tutors. During high school, she opted to attend public school, where she was determined to succeed but struggled academically. She was placed in the LD classes but felt out of place because many of the students were physically handicapped.

When she investigated colleges that would be compatible with her religious beliefs as well as offer special services for the learning disabled, she discovered that Evangel College met both requirements. She and her parents visited the college, talked with the personnel of the Center for Effective Learning (CEL), and opted to send Samantha to Evangel College for her training.

Based on the reported academic history and her ACT composite score of 15, Samantha was enrolled in all the proficiency classes (Basic Algebra, Basic English, Reading Development) and the study skills class, which is a semester-long, three-hours-per-week class teaching distinct study skills. She also elected to take two freshman general education classes.

As a unit of the study skills class, a great deal of time and emphasis is placed on time management and the strategic placement of classes in the available study hours. In other words, study the hardest or least-liked class early in the day and save a favorite class for the last study period at night. Samantha states that this is one of the most important strategies that she could have learned. Since she is concrete in her learning style, it was important that she have some kind of structure for study time. She reported that during high school, she would spend four or five hours nightly studying. As a result of the time management unit, Samantha uses a study schedule consistently, schedules assignment due dates on a calendar, and records daily to-do activities in an appointment book. She reports that this strategy gives her a firm foundation and structure for her academic life.

The use of a calendar to schedule academic activities is often helpful.

Using the skills she learned in the reading development class (SQ3R) and the study techniques learned in the study skills class, she says she spends fewer hours studying and comprehends more in college than in high school.

Another strategy that Samantha finds beneficial is being allowed to take tests for all her classes under a proctor at the Center for Effective Learning rather than with the class. The untimed situation allows her time to focus, read, and think, which relieves a great deal of pressure and tension and results in better test scores. The personnel of the CEL served as liaison to accommodate this strategy for her.

Untimed tests allow students to focus on responses rather than a time limit.

Samantha shows no outward signs of being an epileptic. The seizures are controlled by medication and, while she still has difficulty with writing assignments, she is functioning at a 2.0 grade point average. Her greatest success, she says, is the fact that with the personal counseling received at the CEL, she has overcome her emotions of being a failure and now says, "I'm not an 'A' student but I'm also not an 'F' student."

She has gained so much confidence in her time management skills and study strategies, that she now has time to work two jobs, is president of her floor, and is keeping her grades up as well.

A student with a disability may need counseling to help overcome personal feelings of inadequacy and "differentness."

Samantha graduated in May 1994, with an Associates of Arts degree in Early Childhood Education. She plans to teach in a daycare center upon graduation, and gain some practical experience in the operation of a center with the goal of designing her own daycare center. Her father is associated with a major airline that is considering offering daycare services for their employees. Samantha intends to design and create a center that will be submitted for consideration. She is also considering, at some time in the future, obtaining a bachelor's degree—something she never dreamed she could attain.

Instructional Accommodations for Students
Impacted by Chronic Health Problems

adaptive physical education courses
outlines provided for lectures
alternate location for testing
use of a scribe or notetaker
extended time for tests
tape record lectures
series of short tests
seating location

Chapter 6
TEACHING STUDENTS WITH HEARING IMPAIRMENTS OR DEAFNESS

A student with a hearing impairment or deafness may have difficulties with auditory acuity, ranging from deafness to corrected or partially corrected hearing, or with auditory discrimination. Deficits in auditory discrimination may lead to difficulties hearing sound frequencies or to confusion with certain sounds. A student who is deaf and uses sign language as a first language of communication may have difficulty with the grammatical and syntactical structure of the English language. (Lissner, 1992)

Commonly Associated Disabilities

learning disabilities
auditory agnosia
head trauma
deafness
tinnitus

The establishment of good communication is the foundation of student success.

Here is a list of questions to consider or discuss with the student who is hearing impaired or deaf.

1. What is the student's preferred approach to communication?
2. In what ways can I assist the student, an interpreter, or both to prepare ahead of time? (outline, vocabulary lists of specialized terms, lecture notes)
3. Is my classroom arranged effectively so all class members have eye contact with me and so the interpreter and student can have eye contact?
4. Do I situate myself appropriately in the classroom and speak meaningfully to the student? (lower voice pitch, avoid hand gestures and cigarettes, use facial expressions and body-language for emphasis, and no glare producing light sources)
5. Do I encourage class members to interact meaningfully with the student?
6. How can I clarify key points to the student in class? (notetaker, use of blackboard and overhead projector)
7. If I cancel class, how can I notify the student who must cancel services provided by the interpreter?
8. Are there supplementary materials that may be helpful to the student?

Algebra in a Silent World
by Deborah J. Cochener

Instructors benefit by knowing who to go to and where to go for help.

My initial reaction was one of panic when the disabilities coordinator informed me that I would have a hearing impaired student in my intermediate algebra class the following semester. I had never met a deaf person before and was at a loss as to how to teach someone with whom I could not verbally communicate. Hundreds of unanswered questions raced through my mind.

Modifications in teaching style may be required; however, these are usually easily made and necessitate more of a "common sense" approach than research.

What will I have to do differently?
1. I soon discovered that I could not continue to "talk with my hands." This is a distraction to both the signer and the listener.
2. I *must* pause for student thought and response time. My normal procedure is to talk continually, leaving no "dead air space." Since the signer is not signing from a prepared script, he/she needed some "pause" time to keep up with the lecture.

Will having a signer affect the rate at which I cover the material?
No, in fact, condensing my lecture to allow time for student responses and assimilation, instead of talking continually, actually improved the presentation of my lecture.

How will the hearing impaired student cope with "listening" to the signer and copying the examples on the board?
The visual sense is trained to compensate for the hearing loss; however, it is still difficult to do two tasks simultaneously and be thorough with both. Using a classmate as a notetaker enabled my hearing impaired student to keep up with the notes and the lecture. Brief notes were frequently jotted down to serve as a reminder of a particularly critical point and then later merged with the notes taken by the designated notetaker.

How will the other students handle having a signer in class?
Initially, the other students were distracted by the novelty of the signer. Unlike my hearing impaired student, the hearing students were not able to watch the signer *and* keep up with the lecture examples on the board. By the end of the first week of class, everyone was on task.

OBSERVATIONS

Over the past twenty-one years of classroom experience, I have taught many students for whom English was a second language. It is my observation that by necessity, these students generally spend more quality time outside of the classroom on their assignments than their English-speaking peers. A hearing impaired student is no different from the student for whom English is a second language. The hearing impaired student has learned American Sign Language (ASL) and has also been taught to verbally communicate. In preparation for my algebra class, the hearing impaired student *Frequently* followed two basic procedures. First, both the student and the *students must* signer reviewed the text material that was to be covered in class, *initially spend* working out appropriate signs for the technical terminology that *more time* had no corresponding ASL. Second, the student kept detailed notes *class than their* of questions and concerns in her homework and visited my office *nondisabled* at least once a week to clarify these questions or concerns. Initially *counterparts.* the signer accompanied the student during these office sessions, *However, as* however it frequently proved more beneficial to write brief notes *techniques* interspersed among the lines of the example being discussed than *become "rou-* to communicate through a third person. The signer's sole use *tine" a spirit of* gradually gravitated to "social chit-chat" at the beginning of the *cooperation is* visit. As the semester wore on, the student often came without the *fostered.* signer (sometimes just to chat) because she was comfortable conversing with me through our own contrived means.

HAZARDS

The first hazard encountered was the student's lack of English-language background. From my viewpoint, a deaf student must learn to assimilate in three ways: written English (reading), spoken English (writing) and American Sign Language. Parents who try to shelter a deaf child early in life severely limit all three of these. Growing up, my hearing impaired student had been sheltered from the "outside" world. As a young child she learned to depend on her own "sign language" to communicate with her family. When she began school, she was in the same position as a child who enters our school system speaking only his or her native tongue. My student did learn ASL, but was discouraged at home from trying to verbally talk because her parents thought she sounded stupid and did not want others to think that she was. Thus she entered class, "speaking" the language of ASL and reading English. At the same time, she was enrolled in a developmental English class to remediate her writing skills. A person's writing abilities are closely connected to their fluency with the spoken language. Because this student had not been encouraged to develop the spoken language, her writing skills were weak. The difference between the ASL translation of the spoken word versus the written word often occurred during testing situations or in understanding the wording of an application problem. Thus the question: if the signer signed the written test question, was the ASL interpretation an added advantage that the hearing students lacked?

A good teacher must be able to adjust when unforeseen circumstances occur.

The second hazard was encountered when the signer failed to arrive for class. Our signer was extremely reliable but was absent due to an unexpected illness one day. The substitute signer came but went to the wrong building. What should be done? Much to my dismay, I learned that when the same situation had occurred in high school, the student was made to wait in the hall until the signer showed up! My resolve was that this class would proceed with a minimum of disruption to schedule! I had faced the challenge of condensing my lecture to allow "pause" time for both the students and the signer at the beginning of the semester. If there is no signer the lecture must now be condensed to pertinent points that can be written on the board with the example. My dedication to this hardworking young woman was fierce; I was determined that everyone be on equal footing that day. If I could not write it—I did not speak it. We covered less material than intended, but no one was left out of the discussion. When individuals asked specific questions, students sitting next to the hearing impaired student quickly wrote both the question and the response in her notebook. The class was a team at this point.

The interaction and communication of other students in the learning environment is a part of good teaching practice.

Another hazard occurs when the substitute signer *does* show up. Not having previewed the text material with the student, this substitute had no "signs" for the technical symbols and terminology. As a result, she frequently tried to "finger spell" the words, falling hopelessly behind in the lecture. Unfortunately, I was unaware of this until the lecture was over. The next day the hearing impaired student was in my office. She had read (and reread) the text, worked through the lecture notes taken by the notetaker and worked through examples, writing specific questions beside each note or step that presented a difficulty. In short, she had made accommodations for an unfortunate situation.

Making one's own accommodations is necessary for learning independence.

BENEFITS

As the semester came to a close, my hearing impaired student was earning a solid "B" average in my class and had developed the algebra skills necessary to complete the core mathematics classes. However, all of us learned far more than just algebra that semester. We learned about teamwork, dedication, and perseverance. Attitude and effort are the key to success in any situation. One student enrolled in an ASL class, eager to "speak the language." There were smiles all around the room the day before the final exam as she braved her first attempt at signing. Courageously, the hearing impaired student verbally said "thank you."

Hiding Behind the Hair
by Andra Dorlac

Two years ago, a student was struggling with our U.S. History course, which he needed to complete for missed credit at his high school. In order to graduate that year, he needed not only to pass this course and two others in our learning center at the community college, but all the other courses he was currently enrolled in at the high school. The student seemed to take his work seriously and to be putting forth much effort, but to no avail. He was testing repeatedly to try to achieve the required mastery levels on the modules for this course. At first, we thought the student was having difficulty with reading the questions on the study guides since many of his answers made no sense. Upon administering a standardized reading test, however, it appeared that his reading ability was within normal ranges, so we were truly puzzled. Then, the student happened to mention to an instructor that he was having trouble hearing the audio tapes. Because his hair covered his ears, we had not noticed that he was wearing a hearing aid. This hearing problem proved to be a real disadvantage in this particular course, since the student received most of the instruction through listening to an audio tape in conjunction with a filmstrip.

The student must communicate his needs to the instructor.

I immediately contacted the student's high school counselor to verify the student's auditory disability, only to learn from the counselor that all he knew about this student was that he had a history of failure throughout his schooling and that he was in his fifth year of high school. Upon checking his permanent records and consulting with the school nurse, however, the counselor was able to confirm that the student did indeed have a hearing problem and had been prescribed hearing aids. Since I suspected that learning problems might be compounding this student's difficulties, I recommended to the counselor that diagnostic testing be undertaken. This testing revealed that the student was learning disabled, and he began receiving special services and accommodations at the

Effective documentation of the student's learning history helps the student make appropriate learning decisions.

high school within weeks.

The student and the instructor cooperate and identify ways the student can learn.

To adapt the learning environment for this student in our learning center, I copied the transcripts that the publisher had provided with this audio-visual material so that the student could read (instead of listen) to obtain the needed instruction. Since the student also needed our study skills course, it was necessary to contact that publisher, also, to request the scripts for its audio tapes. Even though the publisher had merged with another company and moved

Timely notice of the need for assistance from outside the college will get the student started off right at the beginning of the course.

to a new location, the service representative agreed to search the files for the scripts and copy and mail them to us free of charge.

Fortunately, this story has a happy ending since this student completed our two courses successfully. In addition, he did well in his high school courses and only needed to finish up one other course with us that summer in order to pick up his diploma. This is a good example of a student who had "fallen through the cracks" in the educational system and was on the verge of dropping out, not willing to face a sixth year of high school. Yet through awareness

Cooperation from various people helped the student to succeed.

and some accommodations in the educational settings, he was able to graduate. He was a different person, with renewed self-esteem, by the time he left our program, and all of us who worked with him are moved every time we retell his story. Recently, we followed up on this student and learned from his mother that he is gainfully employed. She also indicated that he seems to have "come out of

Increased confidence and successful learning strategies will lead to learning independence.

his shell" and no longer feels the need to hide his disability; in other words, the haircut is now above the ears. We can feel good about this success story, but the real value of this experience lies in our continuing to be on the lookout for students who have auditory disabilities and having transcripts available for these students so they are not penalized unnecessarily by the presentation format of some of our courses.

Moving from American Sign Language to English Language Communication
by Meredith Gildrie

As more deaf students enter classes in hearing environments, we need to consider how their deafness impinges on our teaching and their communication. If we are truly dedicated to helping students attain college-level skills, we need to be aware of the obstacles they face and to seek ways to direct them appropriately, so they can develop their skills and abilities.

Recently I have worked with a deaf student in developmental reading and writing courses. Previously I had seen deaf people who seemed to be using standard English. Their finger spelling and *Understanding* gestures seemed to follow English grammar and syntax. Those *the impact of a* who used lip reading as a means of understanding speech ob- *disability helps* viously followed English sentence structure. Knowing of deaf *the student* people rather than knowing a deaf person, I was ignorant of the *appropriate* reality of English as a second language for the deaf. Now I am *strategies for* more aware of the challenges that reading and writing in English *learning.* pose for the deaf, particularly for those deaf from birth.

Most American deaf people use American Sign Language (ASL) to communicate among themselves. For most, it is their first language. It is a separate language, not just a visual version of English. Its vocabulary, or signs, do not correspond exactly to English words. Its grammar and syntax do not match English grammar or syntax. The distinctions between English and ASL makes writing and reading English difficult for the deaf just as writing and reading it are difficult for other people for whom English is a second language.

My student, for example, often does not use articles in her sentences. (ASL has no articles.) She may want to write *court agent* or *judge agent* instead of judge when writing about the person who presides over a trial since that idea takes two signs in ASL. When reading the word *which* in English she has to decide its function since ASL has two different ways of expressing that English word, one to indicate a question and another to indicate a relative pronoun.

Since signs for verbs in ASL do not change tense, my student does not always use appropriate endings to indicate tense. Her natural inclination is to indicate time as a separate element in her sentence. For example, to write "It rained," a word for sign translation from ASL would be "Yesterday rain" or "Past rain." Once a time frame has been established, there is no need for tense indicators in ASL. All verbs are assumed to be in that same time frame. When the time changes, a new time indicator will be mentioned. All actions that follow it are considered to be in that new time frame until a different time indicator is signed. Unless a reading passage uses many direct references to time, the deaf student may have trouble following shifts that are indicated by tense changes.

Although pronouns exist in ASL, they are often presented in the form of signing or pointing toward a location that has been established as the location of a thing. They are not signed separately as often as they appear in English. Certain verbs incorporate the idea of a pronoun in their sign, so ASL users may not automatically use pronouns in their English writing. For example, the concept *to see* is signed by moving two fingers out from the eyes. If that movement goes straight out from the signer, the concept *you* is in the verb. If it goes to the right or left, him, her, or it is included. The concept *help* is signed by placing a fist (thumbside up) on a flat palm. If the sign is moved from the chest forward, the subject *I* and the object *you* are included in the verb. If it is moved from left to right, the sign means "He helps her (him or it)." Since no separate pronoun signs are used in these situations, pronouns may be left out of English sentences as well.

Perhaps differences in syntax create the most difficult problems. In ASL, the most important concepts are usually put first in a sentence. Verbs and question markers often come at the end of a sentence. To communicate "You have to be careful when driving on ice in winter," the deaf may think of concepts equivalent to "During cold car ice skill require." "How do you get to your house from here?" might be written "House go how." These problems in writing and reading lessen as students have more contact with English. However, this takes time, often more time than usual classroom procedures and course time requirements allow.

Since ASL is a visual language rather than an aural one, learning English can be a more difficult task for the deaf than it is for a speaker of another aural language. Although there are conversational-level dictionaries of signs for people trying to learn ASL, I know of no sign to English dictionaries to help the deaf translate and understand English words. Other English-as-a-Second-Language students often learn new words by using their special language dictionaries (English to Spanish, or Spanish to English, for example) when doing class activities or assignments. The deaf can not. Sending them to an English dictionary is only helpful if they already know numerous English words. Even my English-speaking students have trouble deciphering dictionary definitions in their native English, so I know it is not the best solution for ASL signing students. Having a signer in class is helpful, but deaf students can not have a signer with them every time they are exposed to unfamiliar words. They need other ways to learn new English words and usage. Furthermore, the deaf do not have aural exposure to the language to reinforce learning. They can not practice by listening to others. Even if they join in a conversation through a signer, communication is not accomplished in English but in sign. Concepts are signed, not words. Until a person who uses ASL learns finger spelling, the spelling of English words, and the concepts behind those words, that person can not communicate in the English language. They need some way to frequently communicate in English for practice. Deaf students may avoid facing up to the need to learn

English since they can understand and express themselves more easily and more precisely in ASL. They may avoid doing in-class assignments or be totally frustrated by them. Providing for additional, yet supervised, outside-of-class time for language refinement is helpful. This may be in the form of proofreading and editing time in a writing lab before an assignment is graded.

Instructors should consider having some conferences with their deaf students without the aid of a signer after explaining that practice is the purpose of those conferences. Communication is then done through writing. Setting up computer terminal telephone conversations (two-way communication through computer systems) provides language practice. Book talks or study groups among students using e-mail can include the deaf in conversation. This gives practice that does not have to be graded, yet it's connected with course work. Because so much of the world's knowledge is stored and passed on through the written word, the difficulties American deaf students face when English is not their first language cannot be ignored. Their ability to share their insights outside the deaf community is too important to allow us to eschew the challenge of helping them master English.

Support for communication outside of the classroom will enhance the academics of all students.

ACKNOWLEDGMENT

I want to thank interpreters Harriet Beasley and Ray Vaughn for their willingness to share information and ideas regarding this topic as well as to credit Lou Fant's *The American Sign Language Phrase Book* (Chicago: Contemporary Books, 1994) as a source of information for this article. However, any errors present here are solely mine.

Instructional Accommodations for Students Impacted by Hearing Impairments or Deafness

assistive learning device
speak facing student
seating location
sign interpreter
tape recorder
notetaker

Chapter 7
TEACHING STUDENTS WITH INTEGRATIVE PROCESSING DIFFICULTIES

A student with integrative processing difficulties may find problems in spatial orientation like the difference between left and right. Other problems that may be experienced are producing specific motor output from given sensory input (like writing notes in class from a lecture), sequencing information properly, and processing information in a given length of time. The disability is often not visible. (Lissner, 1992)

Commonly Associated Disabilities

attention deficit disorder
dysgraphia and dyslexia
psychological disorder
agnosia and aphasia
learning disabilities
seizure disorders
head trauma
narcolepsy

The establishment of good communication is the foundation to student success. Here is a list of questions to consider or discuss with the student who experiences difficulties with integrative processing.

1. Does the student find it difficult to write or talk about something that has been recently read or listened to?
2. In what ways can testing the student's knowledge be best accomplished?
3. Does the student follow directions better in a quiet area than in a distracting environment?
4. Is the student easily frustrated or angered by homework, class projects, or preparing for and taking exams?
5. Is it difficult for the student to read, write, spell, or use numbers?
6. What does the student's handwriting look like?
7. What would be the most appropriate way to do research and write reports? What options are available to assist the student?
8. Does the student seem unorganized with daily scheduling and with personal belongings or disoriented by unfamiliar situations or surroundings?

Teaching Elementary Algebra to Learning Handicapped College Students: A Case Study
by Deann Christianson and Elaine Werner

At the University of the Pacific (UOP) in Stockton, California, approximately 350 students are placed in developmental mathematics (defined as Intermediate Algebra or below) each year. Of that number, about 10% have learning disabilities. Students who are identified as learning handicapped and who are placed in Elementary Algebra generally have great difficulty completing their course. These students have often had little or no algebra in high school and they exhibit a variety, in both type and severity, of learning disabilities.

Avoidance was a coping strategy that later added to the impact of the student's learning disability.

Terry is one of these students. She came to our university as a transfer student intending to major in elementary education. She was not initially identified as a learning disabled student and in fact had never been assessed. She had managed to avoid mathematics through high school and community college and had used a tutor extensively to complete the little mathematics required of her in the private high school that she had attended. Her initial placement was in prealgebra, which she completed in two semesters. This student had excellent verbal and social skills and was generally a successful college student with a B average. She initially exhibited only mathematics anxiety and avoidance.

Learning strengths were identified.

Serious problems were noted when she attempted the elementary algebra class, a prerequisite for the two courses she needed for her major: a content and methods class for elementary education majors and a statistics class for a general education major. Her retention from the prealgebra class was very slight and seemed to be rote learning. Her anxiety level was increasing and her progress was slow despite an intense work effort. She did not want to use a calculator at all as she thought she "should be able to do this work alone." She had difficulty with signed numbers, variables, and verbally stated problems. At this point, assessment was recommended by the teaching staff. The student seemed anxious to be assessed and shared a more detailed educational history that clearly indicated a need for assessment.

All learning disabled (LD) students at UOP may release to instructors a letter from the school LD coordinator describing the type of learning disability that he/she has and the type of accommodations required. The letter may include the actual assessment report. These letters are necessary to allow the student to receive accommodations in class. Terry's letter and assessment reported a lower than expected IQ score given her college performance (still in the normal range), and several areas of difficulty that clearly were assessed as learning handicaps. The psychologist who tested her was concerned about anxiety interference in the testing but identified quantitative reasoning and recall as areas of disability.

Lack of achievement attributed to learning disabilities may be complicated by a student's lack of confidence.

The staff of the Mathematics Resource Center had developed a series of accommodations for LD students involving both course structure and teaching strategies that are tailored to individual needs. Some of these accommodations and strategies that were used with Terry are described below.

1. *Time accommodations.* A policy allowing for the grade "incomplete" has been developed so that LD students may take more than one semester to complete their self-paced developmental mathematics course. This policy is clearly spelled out in the course policy statement distributed to all students. They are helped to learn how to set reasonable time goals for learning material. Terry was expected to complete the Elementary Algebra material in a full year instead of a semester.

A coalition of support was important to the student's educational goals.

Sometimes LD students cannot complete a unit test or midterm test in the time allocated for class. Students are allowed to take one page of the test at a time and if they are unable to finish a complete test in one sitting, they may return and finish uncompleted pages with no penalty. They may also take tests during an open lab period where two to three hours of time are available. Terry routinely spent two hours taking tests designed to be completed in twenty minutes.

2. *Materials accommodations.* All LD students are required to

use calculators at all times. These calculators must have fraction keys and generalized power and root keys. We recommend a scientific calculator with two variable statistics. LD students are taught to use their calculators gradually in coordination with course material. For some students, we recommend the TI Math Explorer, which is simple to use, has standard fraction notation, allows division with a whole number remainder, and has large brightly colored keys. Terry purchased and learned to use the TI Math Explorer thinking that it would be useful in her teaching experiences. The fraction keys were especially helpful to Terry.

Students with recall and memory disabilities are allowed to use formula cards and notes on all tests. Instructors authorize the use of such aids and help students learn to prepare such cards. Formulas such as the distance formula, geometric formulas, slope, distance, and quadratic formulas are given to students with recall problems. Occasionally, process steps are provided for students who have difficulty recalling the order of problem solving procedures. For example, the following steps were provided for Terry to assist her in recalling the process for solving first degree equations in one variable.

1. Draw a vertical line through the equal sign in an equation to separate the right- and left-hand sides of the equation.
2. Clear the equation of fractions by multiplying each side of the equation by a common denominator.
3. Eliminate any parentheses and combine like terms.
4. Separate variables. Use addition or subtraction to move all variables to the left side of the equation and numbers or constants to the right. (This helps students with right/left confusion by being directive.)
5. Divide both sides of the equation by the coefficient of the variable you are solving for.

Students who require lectures and learn best in that mode are provided with videotapes that they can repeatedly view. The videotapes are available from publishers and are keyed to the texts being used. Terry chose not to use video lectures. Her oral learning ability in mathematics seemed to be low.

Covering textbook pages with colored sheets of plastic may help an LD student read the text. Teachers should keep several color plastic overlays available to test individual students as a possible method of improving reading. Students also may show a preference for using colored paper or low-glare paper for homework. Teachers should provide samples of paper to students to see if reading and writing can be improved. LD students should always use graphing paper and not be expected to draw their own coordinate systems.

Terry preferred low-glare paper and graphing paper but was not helped by colored plastic overlays.

3. *Curriculum accommodations.* For students with severe learning disabilities that interfere with symbolic manipulation in the most profound ways, an adjustment in topics covered is made. Material on algebraic fractions is deleted. Roots and radicals material is shortened and only the quadratic formula is taught as a method for solving general quadratic equations. Equation solving, graphing, and verbal problems are emphasized. Since many of these students are preparing to take statistics, it is these skills that will be most needed. Permission to modify course content in special cases has been given by the Associate Dean of our college. Modification of the curriculum is decided by the staff on a case-by-case basis. Terry was offered the trimmed curriculum but chose to try to complete the standard course.

4. *Teaching Strategies.* More time must be spent teaching organization and neatness in writing mathematics with learning handicapped students. This may include showing the student how to organize a homework binder and how to keep assignment sheets in order. Methods of self-checking are most important as LD students make more than the usual number of "careless errors."

A method of teaching verbal problems to LD students, which has been effective, is to make tables based on the underlying formula (basic sum or difference, distance, interest, mixture, money, etc.) assumed by the problem. Tables help students organize their reading so that the relationships necessary to write equations are most apparent.

When teaching LD students to multiply polynomials, the foil method is not used. Instead, a generalized distributive principle is taught moving from left to right. When factoring of polynomials is taught, trial-and-error factoring is not used. Instead, the method of master product factoring is taught. This method seems much more effective and can be used in all situations. Students are not taught to recognize perfect squares or sums or differences of cubes.

Colored pens or pencils can be used to help discriminate an exponent from a base, a numerator from a denominator, or an operation sign from the sign of a number. Single ballpoint pens with four colors available on them can be helpful.

When teaching equation solving, terms that are to be added or subtracted to both sides of the equation should be written below the initial equation and then added or subtracted. A vertical line drawn through the equal sign helps LD students visually separate the right- and left-hand sides of an equation. An example follows:

$$4x - 7 = 2x + 9$$
$$\quad\; + 7 \qquad\;\; + 7$$
$$4x \quad = 2x + 16$$
$$-2x \qquad\;\; -2x$$
$$2x \quad = \qquad 16$$
$$\frac{2x}{2} = \frac{16}{2}$$
$$x = 8$$

Memory mnemonics are used to help students remember procedural steps. The staff has made up several cue words or stories to help students recall procedure.

All of these teaching strategies were used with Terry. Her recall problems prevented long-term retention of all but the most simple manipulations with variables and equations. She could complete individual units but showed poor retention on cumulative review examinations. She could substitute numbers for variables, solve simple equations, compute with signed numbers, but never successfully completed all of her elementary algebra material. After her assessment and the completion of two semesters of work in algebra, she decided to appeal for a waiver of prerequisites and try her required course. She had not completed the material on graphing, algebraic fractions, radicals, and the quadratic formula. She did however, successfully complete her method and content course with a C. The manipulative material she used in the course seemed to benefit her greatly. She did receive tutoring and support from the Mathematics Resource Center to assist her in completing this course. Her quantitative skills requirement was waived and she is currently attempting to pass the quantitative portion of the California Basic Skills Test so that she can student teach in kindergarten and graduate with teaching credentials.

Finding compensating strategies that lead to success can lead to greater confidence and a willingness to be challenged in new ways.

During the three-year period that Terry worked with the resource center staff, her career goals changed and she is now considering a Master's Degree in Special Education to work with learning handicapped children in the primary grades. She has decided to take statistics, which will meet her general education requirement and is a necessity for graduate school. As a fifth-year senior, she is considering returning to the Mathematics Resource Center to complete the remaining portion of the elementary algebra course.

Finally, it should be noted that not all LD students have difficulty learning mathematics. Some can do excellent work and will major in engineering, science, or mathematics. Other LD students will experience great difficulties and will require a large amount of extra teacher time; but, these students can cope with basic mathematics.

They can usually succeed in a college-level statistics course if they have some of the underlying elementary algebra skills or, as in Terry's case, complete a course for education majors.

LD students are legally entitled to reasonable accommodations and ethically entitled to our best efforts in helping them to succeed at some level in mathematics and in college.

Students with learning disabilities are a diverse group of learners.

I-PLAN: Self-Awareness and Self-Advocacy
by Jorene DeAmicis-Burke

Project Academic Skills Support is a grant-funded program designed to assist college-capable learning disabled students in their efforts to achieve a college education and to become independent members of society. However, we have found that the students with whom we work are sorely lacking in the areas of self-awareness and self-advocacy, making such previously stated accomplishments difficult. To that end, I have found that providing direct instruction in both areas in an actual classroom setting can have measurable and observable effects.

Access to content learning must be supported by learning how to learn.

In the first in a series of four support classes, I address both areas via a curriculum that integrates content instruction with strategy instruction. I begin by presenting the definition of learning disabilities as put forth by the National Center for Learning Disabilities (NCLD). As my students become comfortable with that definition, we examine their documentation from previous testing to determine the exact area of information processing in which they have been diagnosed as having difficulties. From there, we proceed to defining exact learning styles via a series of learning style inventories, including those of Rita Dunn. Armed with this knowledge, we complete a Psychoeducational Profile that addresses individual strengths and weaknesses in a variety of areas. At that point, I introduce the I-PLAN strategy out of the University of Kansas, which emphasizes the importance of inventorying (the "I" of the strategy) strengths, weaknesses, learning preferences, and goals to conference with instructors in order to obtain the appropriate academic modifications needed to eliminate or minimize the impact of an individual learning disability. The rest of the strategy outlines the most efficient means of participating in a conference in order to obtain the specified goals. After appropriate practice, we generalize the idea presented by I-PLAN via individual conferences with me, and at least one other instructor. This same process is reviewed and replayed in the other three support classes with lessening involvement on the part

It is important to specify both long-term and short-term goals with the student.

of our staff and greater involvement on the part of the individual student. Ideally, the psychoeducational profile developed during that first semester is modified and/or improved upon each succeeding semester until that information, too, is internalized to the extent that the form itself is not really needed for reference.

To illustrate this particular approach, we can follow the progress of one of our students who is now completing his degree in Business Administration at a four-year university. Paul came to us after having spent a year out of school on academic suspension because he had continually failed the Basic Skills required courses and had a history of poor attendance as well. He had reluctantly enrolled in our Academic Skills course at the request of the Registrar as a condition of his reentry to Ocean County College. He was resistant, at first, to come to grips with the definition of a learning disability, especially the idea that it is a permanent disorder. However, as other members of the class shared their experiences with academic failures despite varying degrees of effort, Paul began to internalize the definition and get comfortable with it. From there, we moved to his file to "demystify" the technical jargon, and to get an even more precise picture of Paul's cognitive processing problems. Our next step was to determine his learning style and become comfortable with his strengths and weaknesses. We used a number of learning style inventories to determine that Paul was, in fact, an auditory learner. His visual memory skills were very weak, and his short-term memory skills were also a problem. We did determine, however, that his long-term retrieval skills were very good, and his oral language skills were very good, too. As we filled out the Psycho-Educational Profile sheet, he began to realize that there were specific strengths he could call upon to compensate for his weaknesses, and that specific accommodations should begin to make a real difference in his skills. We included such accommodations as utilizing a tape recorder for class lectures, extended time for tests, and books on tape. In addition, we role-played how he would present the need for these accommodations to his instructors. He began to utilize a daily planner, and organized his time spent at the college in a much more organized fashion. He set up meetings with his instructors to present his accommodation needs. He requested a tutor for his more advanced English courses. As these changes were requested and implemented, Paul's self-esteem seemed to soar. He began to speak to groups of students on tour at our campus about the demands of college, especially for students with learning disabilities. He spoke to parents and faculty during scheduled workshops about college-capable learning disabled students. He went out to area schools and

Time management is often one key for success for students with disabilities.

spoke to groups of learning disabled students interested in attending college. To sum it up, he went from an angry, failing young man with a grade point average of 1.5 to a confident, successful young man who graduated from Ocean County College with an Associates Degree in Business with a 3.9 average—all within the space of three years!!

We have learned that once empowered with a better awareness of those strengths, a better understanding of the weaknesses, and a better sense of how to minimize or eliminate the impact of those weaknesses, students take the I-PLAN strategy and "run" with it. This knowledge definitely improves academic performance a great percentage of the time, but the real growth and improvement is more readily apparent in the way the students view themselves so much more positively. This greater sense of self goes a long way toward becoming not only successful students, but achieving the sense of independence necessary to be successful members of society.

Pointing Toward Self-Sufficiency: Working with a Disabled Writer
by Patricia Eney

Steve was the type of student everyone wanted to know. He was a personable young man who worked hard in his classes and had fun after classes. Unfortunately, his academic performance, especially in his major, Economics, was marred by a written language disability.

I met Steve three years ago when I was first setting up Goucher College's learning center, the Academic Center for Excellence (ACE). As an entering freshman, he was tagged by our Admissions Department and Associate Dean as a provisional admittee. To get him started on the right track, our learning disabilities specialist and I assigned him to a peer study skills consultant and alerted his teachers about the accommodations he would be needing. *A coalition of resources was available to the student.*

Learning strengths were identified early.

During that first year, Steve met regularly with his consultant and was a model student. He did his homework, used his time wisely for completing projects and papers, and attended classes regularly. As the year progressed, we weaned him from the consultant meetings until we thought he was able to "go it alone" for his sophomore year. *Efforts were made by the student to become an independent learner.*

During his sophomore year his scholastic progress radically changed. He failed one course twice, received low grades in several others, and generally lost confidence in his abilities. In the first semester of his junior year, he worked with ACE sparingly, meeting several times with the staff professional tutor. Since I was then serving as lecturer in the English Department and Steve was to have two courses in English the second semester (including my own intermediate writing course). I offered to work with him weekly to analyze his problem and suggest strategies to help him improve his writing.

An invitation was extended to the student to provide assistance.

As Steve began to work in my class and in his others, I realized he had several problems. As each problem surfaced, we discussed it and together arrived at a strategy for overcoming it. During this time I was also in contact with several of his other professors, using their input to address Steve's needs.

Understanding the problem and identifying strategies that work lead to success.

Students with a written language disability often cannot even start the composing process. This was true with Steve. As we discussed his various written assignments it was obvious that he understood the assignments and had great ideas for addressing the issues, but the processing facility in his brain would not allow him to write down those ideas in a logical fashion. However, he was able to dictate a working outline to me. From this outline he could then write a draft. We used this procedure at the beginning of the semester and gradually moved to his using a tape recorder to get down his ideas.

Using technology when appropriate can deemphasize the disability itself.

The actual writing of a draft was another of Steve's problems. Along with his language disability, Steve had a slight manual dexterity problem. While his language disability affected his eye-hand coordination, his manual dexterity problem made his writing very hard to decipher. We found that using the computer to complete each part of the writing process circumvented the eye-hand coordination problem and eliminated the handwriting difficulty. Steve would copy his working outline from his tape recorder, take research notes, and write each draft on the computer. Because of how well he did using the computer in his writing, I even suggested to his professors that they allow him to use a laptop when taking essay tests.

As evidenced by his grades' downward spiral his sophomore year, Steve's biggest problem was a lack of self-confidence. He was able to handle the difficulty of his freshman courses relatively well as long as his skill consultant was there to encourage accountability. But with tougher courses his second year, especially in his major, and not having a consultant to encourage him, Steve lost his confidence.

In addressing his confidence problem, I was careful not to fall into a common LD pitfall: in trying to help these students, often we actually harm them by making them more dependent (Jarrow, 1993). Steve didn't need to be dependent; he just needed strategies to succeed. There were three strategies that we used to improve his confidence. Since I had Steve in my writing class, I incorporated two strategies that I use with all my students. First of all, we had an individual conference as he was writing each of his papers. Steve would tell me what he liked about the paper and what he thought needed assistance. Then I would read through the paper, being careful to point out the good points as well as the problem areas. Finally, I would identify one or two areas to work on (i.e., unity, cohesion, documentation). If the paper was very poorly written, I made sure he left with a strong word of encouragement, not chastisement. Steve responded well to these conferences. At evaluation time he wrote, "If not for the conferences, my papers would be somewhere in limbo."

Since the goal of the student is to move toward learning independence, the student must identify problem areas as they arise and apply learning strengths whenever possible.

The second strategy was using an index card to record Steve's writing progress throughout the semester. For the first and last papers of the semester, I included both the good and "needs improvement" areas on the card. However, in order to save space on the card, for the other papers I only noted what needed improvement on the rough draft and final copy. These notations allowed Steve to see how he had cleared up problem areas on each rough draft and how the problems had become less severe as the semester progressed. This increased his confidence in his writing ability dramatically. At the end of the semester, I gave this card back to him after we had discussed his writing improvement in his final conference. He could then use the card as a reference when he had to write papers for other classes.

The final confidence-building strategy came from Steve's Economics teacher. She had observed that he knew the material that was to be included on the first essay exam extremely well when she held the review class, but his exam grade did not reflect this. She decided to test him orally, an idea that suited him very well even though it would have exasperated the typical student. The results were immediate and profound. He went from a D on the first test to a B+ on the second. Even more importantly, his confidence level soared, for her class was the one he had taken twice with another instructor the year before and had failed both times!

There is no set way to help learning disabled students in a writing classroom. The most important point to remember is to help them become as independent as possible. As Steve showed me, LD students need our help to compensate for their disabilities, but mostly they need strategies to become self-sufficient. Every strategy used in the classroom should point toward this ultimate goal of self-sufficiency.

REFERENCE

Jarrow, J. (March, 1993). Developmental Education and the Learning Disabled Student. Workshop given at the annual conference of the National Association for Developmental Education, Washington, DC.

Teaching Writing to Dyslexics
by Sallie Joachim

Whenever teachers meet students whose performance does not match their apparent or measured intellectual capabilities, they experience a high level of frustration. It is easier to dismiss these students by saying they are not trying hard enough rather than to examine the real problem. In reality, these students may be dyslexic. As many as 10 percent of our students may be struggling with dyslexia.

Dyslexia can be defined as a condition in which the brain processes letters and other symbols differently from the standard way. Dyslexia is not an "illness"; it is merely a different way of looking at letters and symbols. If schools did not rely so heavily on reading, dyslexics would not have so many problems. Many dyslexics succeeded in life before a high school diploma became a necessity, and many are successful today outside the academic world along with those who are able to compensate and succeed within it.

Success in the real world is often measured differently from success within the academic world.

One dyslexic student with whom I worked had been regarded as retarded and was struggling to keep up with his studies at Hudson Valley Community College. His writing showed a common problem for someone with dyslexia, as his letters were often backward and the spelling of some common words varied each time he wrote them. However, his writing was surprisingly perceptive, and he spoke intelligently. When I typed his work without mechanical and "spelling" errors and showed it to other readers, they accepted it and were able to evaluate it for its content, which was equivalent to that of other college students. This student learned to write on the computer and use spell check. However, his low self-esteem kept him from trusting his own work and often led him to copying or paraphrasing the ideas of others.

Complete documentation helps the student to succeed.

Communication between the student and the professor often pinpoints problem areas not mentioned in incomplete documentation.

Another student, after experiencing great frustration on his job, decided to try one more time to attend school in order to advance from his menial, low-paying job. When he came to Hudson Valley, he experienced more frustration in his courses, and even though he completed them, he did not view himself as successful. His writing was stilted and choppy because he limited his vocabulary to the words he could spell. When he wrote for me, I supplied the words he wanted to use and suggested he use a hand-held computer speller when he worked alone. He became confident enough to take another composition class. When I last spoke with him, we had a meaningful discussion about his paper on the playwright Tennessee Williams. He seemed pleased with the success he was having in a challenging class.

The student is evaluated on his or her knowledge rather than on his or her disability.

My understanding of dyslexia became clearer when I compared this handicap to the problem I experience of not having a sense of smell. When people talk about the fragrance of a rose in full bloom or the stench of a wet dog I really do not understand. My lack of this sense does not affect my intelligence and unless I disclose it or join a wine tasting group, no one knows the difference. Dyslexics do not look different either; their brains just function differently.

To get some idea of what it means to be disabled, I tried writing with my left hand. Since I am right handed, I found it very awkward and time consuming, and my writing looked a lot like the clumsy handwriting associated with some dyslexic writers. A learning disability can also be simulated by trying to write near a distracting noise. Frequently, disabled students suffer from an inability to ignore environmental noises. They instead must learn to compensate for their difference.

Understanding the student's difficulties is helpful in order to properly identify good learning strategies.

Teachers can help dyslexic students by providing simple written instructions in addition to their usual oral ones. They can provide more charts, diagrams, and outlines on an overhead projector as they lecture. They can also suggest reading material on the same topic written in simpler language. Material can also be presented in forms other than writing. For example, a teacher may use a videotape of a story for discussion as well as expecting students to read it. Reading cannot be eliminated in academic courses, so teachers can help dyslexics by giving directed instructions for reading assignments. Dyslexic writers need help in outlining their work before they begin, and they may always have to rely on a spell checker or an understanding friend for proofreading.

The student needs guidance through ongoing contact with the professor.

My two students experienced success with the help of understanding teachers. Many dyslexics can achieve academic success with effort on their part and understanding on the part of their teachers. It is helpful to know that dyslexia is not a disease but rather a dysfunction that can lead to lack of risk taking, academic failure, and social isolation. Teachers may also find that these strategies will help other students in their classes as well.

Other students benefit from varied teaching practices.

Phil: Recognizing Dyslexia as an Adult
by Arlene Lundquist

I'd like to introduce you to Phil. Phil graduated from Appalachian State University at the end of the fall semester 1993. Phil came to Appalachian as a transfer student from a local community college. He was forty years old, married, had three children, and worked full time.

In order to really appreciate what Phil accomplished, a little bit about his history will help. He had problems all through school, experiencing social promotions until he found himself out of high school and working at a local hardware store. He decided to take some classes at the local community college but was not successful.

Documentation and knowledge of the student's learning history is meaningful and necessary. He did, however, meet his wife there, and they started their family. When Phil's oldest son was in fifth grade and struggling in school, he was tested and diagnosed as dyslexic. Phil realized that his son's characteristics paralleled his own. He went back to the community college and with the help of the learning assistance personnel, was tested and diagnosed as dyslexic. He started over at the community college and literally learned to read. They also got him enrolled with Recording for the Blind, so that he could obtain his textbooks on tape.

In the spring of 1989 I received a phone call from a colleague at the community college about this man that wanted to transfer to Appalachian and "could they come up and visit me." That was the first time I met Phil. I remember being impressed by the questions he asked about the services that might be available. He had an excellent grasp of his needs, and what services it would take to "get him through." Well, Phil came to the university in fall of 1989, and we began to get acquainted. He had self-identified as a student with a learning disability and provided us with documentation of that disability.

Clearly identified educational goals helped the student communicate his learning needs. At the beginning of each semester it is the policy of this office to sit down with each student and, based on their psychological profile and their own input, a course of action for that semester is planned. Phil utilized books on tape, and when a book was not available through Recording for the Blind or the North Carolina Library for the Blind and Physically Handicapped, it was put on tape for him. He utilized tutors, especially for the math courses he was required to take. He also had his exams read to him, and frequently we scribed for him. All of these things would have mattered little, though, if they had not been paired with Phil's consistent pattern of communication with his faculty, regular class attendance, and the desire to "get his degree."

Phil is an inspiration to all who come in contact with him. During his final semester in school, he shared his story with an adult education class at the university, and there was not a dry eye in the room. He is one of the successes a disabled student services coordinator feels very proud of, and yet, the success belongs primarily to Phil, because without his motivation, drive, and belief in himself, he would not have accomplished his goal.

Self-confidence leads to learning independence.

Building Houses: A Case Study of Directed Reading Journals in the Composition Classroom
by Mary Mattson-Scirocco

With arms resting on the podium, I turned my attention to the college freshmen before me. They were at work, including the student who recently had been diagnosed with Attention Deficit Disorder. Watching her pen paused in midair, the other hand pushing a lock of honeyed hair off her brow, I wondered how this middle-aged woman had coped with the academic frustrations she shared in my office the week before. Without symptoms of hyperactivity, Maureen, like other undiagnosed students with learning disorders, had been labeled lazy or slow in English classes because of her inability to stay focused on reading assignments and other schooling tasks.

Our conversations about this concern began early in the quarter when she had been elated by a technique using reading journals in the classroom. With the strategy, based on Stauffer's (1970) work, I divided a text into sections based on structural breaks: the title, the introduction, time shifts, subject shifts, and the closing idea. At those points, students paused in their reading and responded to questions asking them to anticipate what may happen next in the text, to adjust their expectations according to what had occurred, and to respond personally to lines or events in the scene. Originally, my intention had been to encourage students to slow down their reading and attend to details.

A carefully developed teaching tool for all students may be the key to success for students with disabilities.

READING JOURNALS AS COMPREHENSIVE TOOLS
For Maureen, these journals meant more than a means to draw her attention to details; they amplified her comprehension during reading, a problem that had haunted her in past English classes. Maureen wrote, "I never could seem to remember the points; then I would have to go back and almost have to reread it all over again, but it was like I just couldn't remember how I had experienced it. I could read it, but it just didn't seem like it would make a wrinkle on my brain or something."

*Using diverse
teaching tools
to meet various
learning styles
individualizes
the learning
process.*
With the journal strategy, Maureen noticed that the questions "woke up your senses to be on the look out for something"; writing during reading helped her to stay focused. By breaking the text into sections, she was able to read one part at a time, recording what she found important in a written response.

Instructor's Question: "What do you feel is the most significant line or word in this section?"

Maureen: " 'I stopped judging him years ago,' I feel is the most important line in this section. Wouldn't it be a fabulous world, if no one ever judged another person? Maybe there wouldn't be any homeless people on the street. Maybe the young man at school wouldn't feel rejected because he couldn't wear the latest styles. What about the young girl down the street everyone calls a tramp? Maybe she wouldn't feel like an outcast. Maybe if we didn't judge one another there would be more harmony in the world."

Instructor's Question: "What is your reaction to the end of this essay? Mention significant passages and explain your feelings."

Maureen: "I feel Mr. Rooney was so right when he said, 'A person can be so many different things.' Like the axe murderer who dropped bread crumbs from his cell window to feed the birds, bad people do good things at other times. People make decisions about other people just like Mr. Rooney made it clear that Fred Friendly was his friend, and he accepted him with his good and bad traits. There were two people who had very different opinions about his friend—one was a bad opinion and one was a good opinion. As with mountains, opinions, after being formed, are hard to change."

These two excerpts from one of her entries exemplify the ways the journal acted as a record of the reading experience. Maureen noted lines that were significant to her, such as the one about judging other people. Then she went on to explain the meaning this line had to her by giving examples of a student in her class and a young woman living on her street. By recording her thoughts as she shifted from text to self and then back to text, Maureen found she could recall the work and her interaction with it. As stated above, she felt as a student with an Attention Deficit Disorder that reading didn't seem to make a wrinkle on her brain. Now she had a record of the wrinkle, one that she maintained "deepens the memory."

GENERATING IDEAS

Another advantage of the journal that Maureen cited in our conversations pertained to her problem of inventing focused ideas for a paper. She recalled the frustration she had felt when past instructors informed her it was time to generate a topic for an essay. "I had more ideas than I was able to transfer into words, but often the ideas were hit or miss, sort of like reaching for something in the dark."

With the reading journal, Maureen's commentary included context and a focus from which she could plan her work. After reviewing the entry cited above, Maureen contemplated choices of topics for a paper. She indicated two topics, both strong possibilities, that she could have chosen for a short essay: a narrative of the effects of judgment on the girl down the street or an essay of how those who judge are often myopic in their vision. Maureen wrote, "The journal was like a blueprint. I had to come up with the way to organize it, but the blueprint was there. I just had to fill it in. The journal gave information in black and white that you had thought while reading it, and then you could go back and say, 'Oh, yea, I remember how I felt when I read this,' and what I was picturing or thinking about at the time, and then it would blend all together." As a writing strategy, the reading journal gave Maureen an initial focus for her paper.

The instructor helped the student to identify successful learning strategies.

FIRST STEPS OF THE WRITING PROCESS

Most important to Maureen was the fact that the journals helped her to see how writing is a process that entails a logical, recursive progression. In the past, essays that she had written were "jumbled or sidetracked" compositions for which she had received low scores. She compared her earlier papers with the results of building a house in a ramshackled fashion. "I guess it was like trying to build the attic before you would build the basement, and paint it even before you put on the siding." Because Maureen had no record of her reading experiences to use as idea generation, she had tried to write at random without invention or planning. With the journal as a guide, she maintained, "It was not easy, but you could go; you had something to kind of like make that first step."

CONCLUSION

The reading journal was not a panacea for Maureen's struggle with Attention Deficit Disorder. But it did provide her with a means to record her experiences with texts, to begin generating ideas for her writing, and to understand some of the stages of the writing process. For someone who had dealt with failure after failure in English classes, this was a step forward. As Maureen mused, "After I found out I had an Attention Deficit Disorder, and I began taking Ritalin, it was like I could see for the first time, but there was also the pain of mourning the other half-century of my life that had come before the diagnosis."

Success increases self-confidence.

REFERENCE

Stauffer, R. (1970). *The Language-Experience Approach to the Teaching of Reading*. New York: Harper & Row.

Instructional Accommodations for Students Impacted by Integrative Processing Difficulties

reasonable tardiness/absence
more frequent deadlines
develop study schedule
extend test time
supplement text
tape recorder
relocate test
meet weekly
notetaker

Chapter 8
TEACHING STUDENTS WITH MOBILITY IMPAIRMENTS OR MOTOR CONTROL DIFFICULTIES

A student with a mobility impairment may have difficulties with physical barriers like stairways or long distances between buildings on campus. Difficulties may also be experienced in writing by hand, walking, and/or using the standard apparatus in a given laboratory situation. (Lissner, 1992)

Commonly Associated Disabilities

cardiovascular disorders
muscular dystrophy
traumatic injury
cerebral palsy
head trauma
paraplegia
arthritis

The establishment of good communication is the foundation of student success. Here is a list of questions to consider or discuss with the student who has a mobility impairment or motor control difficulty:

1. Does this student need help with notetaking during class? Would a tape recorder be appropriate to use in class?
2. Is it possible for me to reduce the amount of writing in class by using handouts and other supplementary materials?
3. Does the student need extended time for a test or assignment because of handwriting difficulties? Does the student need a computer in class for notetaking and other writing assignments?
4. Is it appropriate for this student to be tested orally, by tape, or with the use of a scribe?
5. Is the classroom arranged effectively so that the student can access a desk from a wheelchair or situate a wheelchair without blocking emergency exits? Do I need to make appropriate changes in a laboratory situation?
6. Are all class activities accessible to the student? Do I need to notify the student in advance if the class is canceled?

Angela: Capitalizing on Individual Strengths
by Jennie Preston-Sabin

The student asked for help from the appropriate office.

Advanced preparation is important to the student who should not miss class.

Student-faculty rapport is often essential to understanding and building on the student's learning history.

The coordinator of disability issues came to my office prior to the start of a new semester to inform me that I would have a student in my class who had "a mobility impairment." My first concern was that Angela would be unable to attend her first basic math class because it was located in an inaccessible location. After I made arrangements to change classrooms, which caused Angela to miss the first few days of class, get a table for her to use rather than a traditional desk, and position the table so that she had a clear view and other student's views were not impeded—I was ready to begin instructing Angela! Based on everything I knew, I had provided Angela's accommodation. Well, as the weeks progressed, it was clear that Angela's disability was not a mobility impairment. Through weekly appointments, I eventually discovered that Angela has cerebral palsy and her ability to learn math was perhaps being influenced by physical difficulties involving eye-hand coordination and learning disabilities involving the nervous system. This began my four-semester teacher-student relationship with Angela. She is a traditional-age student who was told in high school that she would never make it in college. Her high school preparation was clearly not for attending a four year college.

How has it been possible for Angela to move toward her high goals, in fact, the goals deemed impossible by a former high school algebra teacher? The real story behind Angela is a mother and her family's "can-do" attitude. They were able to nurture and develop this same attitude in Angela. Despite the lack of benefits from regular college prep courses, Angela came to college prepared to succeed. For Angela, the most important thing that Austin Peay provided her was the opportunity to achieve and the faculty in the Developmental Studies Program who could provide appropriate guidance to fill the gaps necessary for firm academic preparation. Angela and I eventually realized that her excellent verbalization skills and her social interaction skills were the strengths she needed to capitalize on in order to get her through the necessary mathematics classes. This is where using study skills benefited her the most in mathematics. She learned to effectively use two-column notetaking. For Angela, the written words in the left column had more meaning than the examples found in the right column. Using notecards also helped her to organize her thoughts so that she could make a memory dump before doing a test. In addition, she read the textbook out loud so that she could hear herself verbalize and focus on the big picture. The other major thing that benefitted Angela was a testing accommodation that slowly developed over five semesters and is now a readily accepted instructional accommodation in the general education core mathematics classes. To begin with, Angela took tests the same way every other student did. After you work so closely with someone you begin to notice things and I slowly noticed that Angela was not writing down the same things she was verbalizing from one line to the next. By her fifth semester, she made fairly smooth transitions into her remaining mathematics classes and was accommodated during testing situations through the use of a scribe. This scribe was an upper-level mathematics student trained specifically to work with Angela on a mathematics test. By using the scribe, Angela was able to verbalize her knowledge of skills and that knowledge could be mirrored in written form for the professor to grade.

Recognizing and using learning strengths is essential.

The student's support was a network of resources readily available on campus.

Angela has now graduated from Austin Peay. She clearly represents the best of the learning and teaching processes. Individual strengths of the student must always be a factor in the classroom. For students with disabilities, individual strengths provide the framework for academic achievement and for learning independence.

Test Accommodations: The Balancing Act
by Jacqueline Robertson

It is the first day of classes at the university. Phil, who is an eighteen-year-old visually impaired student, is sitting next to Tammy, a mother of two who is learning disabled. Phil is also across from Todd, a thirty-five-year-old quadriplegic. Other than the three of them attending a meeting offered by the Office of Disabled Student Development, what could they have in common? More than they realize.

They are all eligible for special services from the university pertinent to their disabilities. The question is not, "Will services be provided?" but "How can the university meet their diverse needs?" One area in which all three students will need accommodations is with fair and appropriate testing. Phil will need a reader and a scribe. Tammy will need extended time, and possibly a reader. Todd will need a scribe. The testing accommodations should match the recommendations reported in the student's diagnostic report, which has been reviewed and kept on file in the Office of Disabled Student Development.

A coalition of support for students is essential to their educational goals.

Test accommodations vary from the instructor's office, to an empty classroom, to an academic assistance center. Options of placing the student in a hallway or allowing him/her to bring a friend as a reader are inappropriate settings. Since most schools have some form of academic assistance, administering the tests in a learning center setting is logical.

The coordinator of proctoring needs to be knowledgeable about disability issues that include maintaining academic standards while at the same time tailoring the situation to meet the specific accommodation described in the student's diagnostic report. This balancing act must judiciously be maintained. Suggestions for testing within a Learning Center are set forth.

Policies and procedures must be clearly documented and understood by all in order to maintain the integrity of the course while providing the appropriate accommodation for the student.

Prior to testing, the following conditions need to occur:

1. Eligibility has been confirmed by the office of Disabled Student Development.
2. The student has asked the instructor for an accommodation.
3. If the learning center is the desired location for the accommodation, the student has scheduled the appointment at the same time that the test will be given to the class.
4. The coordinator of proctoring services in the learning center has discussed the procedures with the professor, when requested.
5. The student and professor are given the policies in writing.
6. The professor delivers the test the day before the testing.
7. Test proctors have received training.

At the time of testing, fair accommodations occur through:

1. Remembering the professor's standards are paramount where test security is concerned.
2. Having the student place bookbags, and so on, in a specific area.

3. Proctoring tests with different personnel than the student's academic tutors.
4. Clarifying procedures, but not concepts or vocabulary words.
5. Providing extended time, but not unlimited time for the test.
6. Using adaptive equipment when possible.

The completed test is placed in an envelope, properly addressed, sealed, taped, and signed over the tape by the coordinator of proctoring services. A student employee of the learning center then hand delivers the test to the instructor's office. Record keeping, contacts with the instructors, and "what if" scenarios are but a few of the additional considerations that need to be incorporated into this model.

Phil, a telecommunications major, is taking a class in which his professor is testing the class twice a week. In this case, Phil attends the class to hear the lectures, then at the time of the test, walks to the learning center for his test. The professor sends the test to the coordinator of testing via electronic mail. It is printed from the computer and administered to Phil. Even though he is congenitally blind, he is computer literate. Phil completes the essay portion on the computer, thus sending it, via computer, back to his professor.

Phil, Tammy, and Todd all play active roles in obtaining the services appropriate to them. Establishing eligibility, discussing accommodations with professors, contacting the learning center, setting appointments for testing, and taking the tests at the scheduled times are all essential steps for the student. Each interaction the student has in which he/she must independently assume responsibility builds confidence. This feeling of success empowers the individual to more confidently approach future educational and employment opportunities.

Successful strategies are a part of lifetime learning.

Instructional Accommodations for Students Impacted by Mobility Impairments or Motor Control Difficulties

change class—advance notice
adaptive physical education
sufficient space for seating
testing alternatives
laptop computer
notetaker

Chapter 9
TEACHING STUDENTS WITH SOCIAL BEHAVIOR DISORDERS OR DIFFICULTIES WITH CONSISTENT PERFORMANCE

A student with a social behavior disorder may act impulsively while another student may experience difficulty with consistent performance or have trouble keeping appointments. (Lissner, 1992)

Commonly Associated Disabilities

arrested substance abuse
psychological disorders
Tourette's syndrome
learning disabilities
seizure disorders
head trauma
lupus

The establishment of good communication is the foundation of student success. Here is a list of questions to consider or discuss with the student who acts impulsively or who has difficulty performing consistently.

1. Does the student participate in class discussions and articulate well but respond poorly on a written test? In what ways can I make sure that I am testing the knowledge of the student accurately?
2. Does the student misinterpret or have difficulty understanding my tone of voice or body language, which may help to emphasize key points?
3. Does the student appear to be anxious, fatigued, apathetic, restless, and so on? When does this seem to occur?
4. Does the student talk out of turn, speak loudly or rudely, stand too close, or interrupt conversations? When should I overlook this and when is it necessary to deal with it when classroom instruction is disrupted? What is the procedure for this?
5. Does the stress of taking a test seem to cause the student difficulty in comprehensión? Would extended time limits be appropriate? Would relocating the test make a difference?

Helping Learning Disabled Students with Mathematics
by Katherine W. Creery

Russell was a severely learning disabled student who had been in special education classes during his public school education. During high school, he had been a resource student with his math and English classes in the resource room with a special education teacher. He had learned coping strategies for all subjects except algebra, which he had attempted all four years in high school.

Documentation and suggested arrangements serve as a starting point for the professor and the student.

Russell brought a form from the Office for Students with Disabilities showing his disabilities, and the accommodations that he would probably need to be successful in the class. This included front-row seating, extra time to take tests in a private room, and taping class lectures. It did not include any information as to how learning disabled he was or that he had attempted this class four times in high school and twice at the university.

I did have him sit in the front row so that he not only had a good view of the board, but would not be distracted by the other students in the class. He said that he did not benefit from taping the class, it just did not make any sense to him when he went back to study.

An invitation for learning assistance was extended to the student.

I asked him to set up an appointment to talk to me in my office. He always had an excuse for not making or keeping these appointments. He passed the first chapter test with a C, but failed the second and third tests. After the third test he did come see me.

He started our meeting with statements as to why I would not be able to help him. He told me that he could not do algebra because it did not make sense to him, and that every teacher thinks he/she has the successful method for teaching algebra to him. Actually they just confused him more, by making him try to learn a new scheme to do the work.

I pointed out that what he was doing was not successful and he had nothing to lose by working with me. We compromised—he would try my suggestions for one week. I had already analyzed his old tests and had heard his statement that algebra did not make sense to him, but arithmetic did. I felt that he was not able to discriminate between the different symbols, numbers, and letters. *Learning* I started by copying a problem on a sheet of plain paper with extra *occurs when* space between each term and sign in the algebra problem. It *dialogue and* helped a little. Then I copied it again on unlined paper; this time I *feedback takes* wrote it in large characters. It helped a little more. Then I took a *place. This* wide red marker and marked over the equal sign and again *often requires* explained the use of the sign. Now I was seeing some real *compromise.* progress, but he was getting positive and negative signs wrong, as if the negative signs were not even on the paper. I used a wide blue marker and marked over each negative sign. This time he tried the problem, and got very close. Next I got a piece of light yellow unlined paper, and once again I put a problem in large print, making the equal sign in red and the minus sing in blue. He worked it correctly, and then told me that he then could see what I meant about an equation having two sides with terms having different signs.

Before he started his homework, I asked him to go by an office supply store and get a couple of sample sheets of different pastel colors. He was to use them to do his homework the way we had just done it. At his next class meeting, he told me that a light gray really helped. As the semester progressed, we changed what was put in markers. The key concept was identifying what he needed to mark boldly.

Russell had another problem that had to be overcome. He was unable to copy a math problem from the textbook accurately. After trying several things, we came up with a simple solution. He was to place a post-it note above and below each problem before he tried to copy it. This prevented him from getting this problem *Ongoing* mixed up with any other one. This same method was used with the *meetings* answers in the book. He even marked the answer page by using *provided* another post-it note. He just left a little of the note showing above *opportunities* the page. He found that one piece of the note paper would last for *for identifying* weeks. *appropriate*

His tests and final exam were written in large print with only *learning* one or two problems on a sheet of paper. The problems were writ- *strategies.* ten in a different color ink, unless they were typed, so the problem could be quickly distinguished from his work. If the problems were long when written out, the paper was turned sideways to fit it on the paper. He supplied the colored paper for the test, and it was his responsibility to write over the symbols with colored markers.

In the beginning it took a lot of time in changing the writing instrument. But as he mastered the concept he was able to drop a lot of what he marked in different colors. On some of the tests he used no color except for the colored paper.

When I would work a problem on the board, I used two pieces of colored chalk to emphasize the step being worked on (I had several other students tell me how much this helped them). Russell was unable to copy the problems from the board, but was able to explain the methods I had just used to his tutor. With the tutor using the same methods, Russell did not get confused by different methods. I had arranged a meeting with Russell, his tutor, and myself as soon as I could after finding the methods that worked well for Russell. While we talked, I had Russell work some problems so that the tutor actually could see how to work with him.

Training tutors about effective learning strategies is an important part of the college's coalition for student support.

Russell made a C on the next test, and an A on the final test. He was not able to pass the final, but made a very good showing considering we were over halfway through the course before he came to my office for help.

Russell did repeat the course the next semester, using all of the methods that had proven to be successful and did pass the course with a strong C. He took Algebra II, with another instructor, and did well on the old material, but was unable to keep up with all of the new material because of the faster pace of Algebra II. As of now, he has not retaken the course.

Remember, Russell has a very severe learning disability. Most of your students will only need to use a few of the above suggestions. Start with one and see what happens, and add others only as needed. Listen to your students, they will be able to tell you what works for them. Under no circumstances, force them to use any method that they do *not* think works for them after trying it for a couple of examples. They will just label you as another "know-it-all" teacher" who thinks he/she knows all of the cures for their learning disabilities. These methods have been successful when used with other learning disabled students, and with students who have problems that are not severe enough to be classified as learning disabled. The best part of this method is that it takes no special equipment, and not too much extra work on the part of the teacher.

Students actively involved with learning how to learn will improve their achievement.

Working with Recovering Chemically Dependent Students
by Joan Essic

James is a 43-year old recovering alcoholic and is a college senior. He has been sober for four years, was very active in Alcoholics Anonymous (AA) for about a year and a half, then stopped attending meetings. He came to Disabled Student Services as a referral from Vocational Rehabilitation Services. He initially described himself as having problems with motivation and focusing on his studies. Questioning brought out that he was depressed and very isolated. He indicated that he was in recovery during the initial interview and stated that his current problems had nothing to do with his alcoholism.

Some of the more common hidden disabilities are those associated with chemically dependent students. These students are encompassed by disability legislation.

Leslie is a 22-year-old woman, a college junior, who is a recovering cocaine addict and has a learning disability. She was quite open with the counselor about having been addicted to cocaine, and having had to drop out of school several years ago for treatment. She is very active socially and reports drinking alcohol, "but not much, just with friends." Her grades are poor and she attributes this to her learning disability, rather than her primary focus on social life and her alcohol use. She reports attending a few AA and Narcotics Anonymous (NA) meetings after treatment but "they were not for me. I don't do coke any more and don't intend to."

Mark is an older student, in his late thirties, who has a physical disability. He has returned to college in order to change to a less physically demanding career. He has been in recovery from alcohol dependence for about eight years, attends AA several times a week, and is very active in that twelve-step program. He has little self-confidence in his academic abilities and is currently making Ds or Fs in three of his four classes. He reports difficulty with concentrating and remembering details. He also has difficulty with motivation.

Support systems outside the classroom may be crucial for learning to take place.

Appropriate accommodation plans are given to the instructor while treatment is handled by an appropriate professional who is apart from the teaching faculty.

These three cases are typical of the types of students we may see today coming through the doors of Disabled Student Services offices across the country, and of the initial information they provide to the college or university. With the advent of Section 504 and its inclusion of psychiatric disabilities, individuals who are recovering alcoholics and drug addicts are entitled to our services, as with any other psychiatric or mental impairment.

As drug awareness has increased over the last eight to ten years, more and more individuals are seeking treatment and recovery. A growing number of these are young—college-age or even younger. These students may have been addicted to alcohol, cocaine, crack, heroin, marijuana, other drugs, or may have been polydrug abusers or addicts. Addiction cuts across every social class, family system, and race.

In addition to the traditional college-age student, we are seeing dramatic increases in the return to college and university campuses of older students who are coming back to begin or complete their educations, or to change their careers. Among these students are also recovering people, many of whom may have been using or drinking since their early teens. These students may carry not only the burdens common to traditional college-age recovering individuals, but the added difficulties of severely impaired coping and social skills, physical or mental impairment as a result of the drugs and/or alcohol, and life problems that may affect their roles as students.

Interactions between professors, counselors and students are confidential.

It is inevitable that these students will be a part of almost every academic counselor's caseload. The counselor needs some basic education about alcohol and drug-related issues for students that is beyond the scope of this subchapter. What is suggested here are both some important questions to ask in initial interviews with students to ascertain if the issue of chemical abuse or dependence is a concern, and some typical problems and strategies for resolution.

The professor does not need to know the specifics of the student's chemical dependency only his accommodation responsibility.

In the interview, it is essential to ask if the student drinks or uses drugs of any type. This must be done nonjudgmentally and almost casually. Questions may be inserted when asking about diet and sleep habits and justified in the context of learning about the student's overall living patterns. It is essential that it be made clear that the information is confidential and it will not be used against them. If good rapport has been established and the student is in recovery rather than using actively, he or she will usually give an honest reply.

For students who report that they are actively drinking or using, attempt to discover what they are using, when, and how much. Always assume that the answer is underestimated. For these students, it is important to help them look realistically at their drug of choice, alcohol included, and whether or not that usage is impairing their academic performance. These students also need some education on the effects of alcohol and drugs. It is a fact that many students drink or use socially with no personal or academic problems resulting. It is also a fact that a significant number who drink or use heavily will become addicted. The most frightening fact is that alcoholism or drug addiction, left untreated, is always fatal. (Alcohol may take as few as four or as many as thirty years to become full-blown; cocaine and crack addiction has been known to occur after two to three uses.) If the counselor determines that the pattern the student describes (or if it becomes apparent later that alcohol or drug use) is affecting the student's life, academically or otherwise, appropriate referrals should be made.

For the student who has been addicted and is no longer using, there are a number of things that are important to know:

1. How long has he/she been clean?
2. What drugs did he/she use, for how long, and at what levels? (I usually ask for amount and frequency.)
3. Is the person active in AA, NA, Cocaine Anonymous (CA), or another twelve-step program?
4. Is he/she in any type of counseling?
5. What problems has the student experienced during recovery that might affect his/her college performance?

Among the problems that these students may report, or that the counselor may become aware of during subsequent sessions, are the following:

1. Compulsive behavior
2. Depression
3. Isolation
4. Anger
5. Feeling singled out and mistreated
6. Resorting to escape into other addictive behaviors
7. Blaming behaviors
8. Lack of motivation
9. Lack of age-appropriate coping and social skills
10. Rigid, black-and-white thinking patterns

Sound common? Of course they do, but for students who have been addicted to alcohol and other drugs, these problems may require slightly different or altered strategies.

The first thing I try to do with anyone who is in recovery is to recommend active participation in a twelve-step program. This offers a support system and a secure, nonusing base of peers for social interactions as well as continued education. It can also help counter a tendency toward isolation. In addition, these groups offer a safe place to practice social skills. While attendance cannot usually be enforced, participation is strongly and consistently encouraged. I would also encourage any academic counselor working with this clientele to attend several open AA or NA meetings so that they will know what they are referring to.

During each session that I work with the student, I will in some way check out both meeting attendance and the emotional state of my client. I am constantly alert to the problems mentioned earlier (some of which signal what is called dry-drunk syndrome: a state in which all of the emotions and behaviors of alcoholism may surface even though the individual is not using). If I become aware of the presence of any of these problems, I will verbally explore what is going on with the individual.

The behaviors and problems created during the addictive process do not miraculously stop or change when a person gets into recovery. He or she must rebuild those areas (such as unlearned social or coping skills), work to alter behaviors (tendencies toward compulsivity, explosive anger, or blaming, etc.), and develop strategies for dealing with moods, emotions, and lack of motivation.

The academic counselor has a many-faceted task. She is not a therapist; but while focusing on academic problems, she must take into account those problems that affect the student's ability to study and succeed. When the problems, such as depression, compulsivity, or coping skills are severe, the student should be referred to the counseling center for therapeutic work, but the academic counselor must still have strategies available to aid the student in his or her day-to-day academic endeavors.

Many of the strategies crossover and are used for a variety of problems. The following are among the ones I have found most useful with this particular group of students:

1. *Depression.* Regular twelve-step meeting attendance. Day-to-day concrete plan of action. Interaction and involvement with others (study groups, clubs, etc.). Affirmations. Uplifting reading or tapes. Exercise. Relaxation. Meditation. Short, systematic periods of study. Priority lists. Realistic goals.
2. *Anger.* Opportunity to ventilate with counselor. Journaling. Exercise. Relaxation methods geared toward relieving impulsive anger. Looking for ways to channel the anger productively. Reality testing.
3. *Isolation.* Often with depression. Twelve-step meetings. Concrete plans that include meeting with others. Getting out of the room (i.e., study in library or other places with people around). Limiting amount of time spent alone (i.e., can't close myself in room until 10 P.M.— out by 9 A.M.). Involvement in helping project of some kind. (The plan to study among other people and be involved daily with some group activity can be extremely helpful.)
4. *Blaming behaviors.* The counselor must be gently confrontational with this one. She must help the client reality-test and set boundaries for appropriate behavior. ("It's the teacher's fault. She wasn't clear." Indicates the need for a future plan that encourages the student to determine what information he needs and how to ask for it.)

5. *Escaping into other addictive behaviors.* Be alert to indicators that the student is overdoing (i.e., I assigned one student a period of relaxation every day, the student tripled it, did it "frantically" every day for a week, then burned out and didn't want to continue). Recovering individuals have a tendency to act as if "this is THE answer" and pursue a new technique or strategy avidly, and overdo, then become discouraged. They must be taught pacing. Work on a balance in every area. Create a plan that focuses not only on academics, but includes time for other activities. Concrete plans that allow for flexibility are extremely helpful (such as time logs, clearly planned but with flexible trading allowed). Also be aware that a person who has been addicted is at great risk to become addicted to another chemical.

6. *Compulsive behaviors.* Similar to above, but with this issue more emphasis is placed on flexibility and the ability to "not be perfect." Limit the behavior. (You can only work out for thirty minutes daily. Study for one hour, then take a break for thirty minutes. In the first draft, don't stop to correct the spelling, etc.)

7. *Lack of age-appropriate skills.* At the point an individual begins to use any kind of mood-alterant heavily, his or her social and coping-skill development grinds to a halt. Consequently, you will encounter students in their thirties and forties who began using and drinking in their early teens and who, although no longer chemically dependent, are at a loss when interacting with peers or when coping with the stresses of normal college pressures. Among the strategies and techniques that work with this are education (Let me show you how to use your body language when approaching your professor. What might you have said that would have let him know you needed help?), role-playing, assigning reading material, small group skills-building (many learning-disabled and physically-disabled students share this lack of social skills). Coping skills can also be taught through the same methods as well as through discussion of alternative options for dealing with situations and the consequences of each.

8. *Lack of motivation.* Very concrete plans of achieving goals. Time-logs. Priority-setting (with a limit on the number of items to be accomplished). Setting goals and breaking down minutely. Daily review of accomplishments. Built-in rewards. Exploration by student and counselor of how to increase motivation and reduce self-defeating behaviors for this specific class, subject, project, etc. The more concrete and broken down, the better.

9. *Rigid black-and-white thinking patterns.* This is by far the most common problem of recovering chemical dependents. The student must be taught how to generate options and recognize diverse viewpoints. I facilitate this process with such strategies as challenging the student's limited ideas, teaching the student to brainstorm options, and encouraging him/her to consult others and gather ideas.

While this is a far from extensive list of special problems encountered with this population, I hope that it may be helpful in increasing awareness of some of the most common issues, and some methods of addressing them.

Helping Students with Attention Deficit Disorder
by Paula A. Gills

I knew Rick was going to present a different challenge the moment he walked in the door to the Learning Support Center (LSC). He was "hyper" in his physical mannerisms, had trouble making eye contact, did not communicate verbally with ease, had a negative and somewhat angry "air" about him and, generally, did not seem comfortable about being at "that place" where special academic services were handled. I had not anticipated what I now

All students need support, the level differs from student to student.

observed based on the testing report I had received prior to his enrollment; all it had indicated was a mild, vague learning difficulty that did not qualify for services under PL 94-142 in his home state. However, it was clear to me from the achievement scores in reading and writing that he was far below where he would need to be to manage college work without maximum support. I noted, as well, a pattern familiar to me in his WISC-R (Wechsler Intelligence Scale for Children-Revised) scores: The comparatively low Arithmetic, Digit Span, and Digit Symbol scores (all measures of ability to attend, in part) pointed to the probability of a high distractibility factor in his learning style, perhaps to a disabling degree.

Persistence is often the key to discovering solutions.

In our introductory conversation, Rick could provide little insight into his learning style or needs, seeming somewhat hostile to my persistent questioning—he did not want to admit to having any "problems" with schoolwork or personal issues. I asked to see some

Time management and study skills are critical for academic success.

of his writing from the class notes he had taken so far; it was almost illegible, and his thoughts were disorganized. He had come to work on a paper for English, referred by his professor, and that, too, showed the same problems as well as underdeveloped topic areas. I asked about time management and study skill strategies. He had none and had not the slightest idea as to how to learn and

Know when to terminate a meeting and when to continue.

practice them. His continual distraction and impulsive responses during our talk made it difficult and frustrating to make much headway, and his growing discomfort with my inability to immediately take expert control and "fix" things for him was bordering on an angry outburst. Ultimately I ended the session and had him reappoint.

In the interim, I called his mother and learned that his testing, performed in the tenth grade, did little to help him in high school;

he was largely left to struggle on his own. Family turmoil, frequent moves, a childhood accident resulting in oxygen deprivation—all these factors emerged in our conversation about Rick, as did her concern that he had a great deal of difficulty following through on tasks and seemed, generally, to be an unhappy young man. I told her that we might try to convince him that further testing would help us, particularly if we were dealing with an undiagnosed attentional disorder (he was clearly presenting a lot of the classic behavioral symptoms of Attention Deficit Hyperactivity Disorder [ADHD]). She had no resources to do this, but Rick's father did, and she said she would contact him. In the end, it took all of us two years to convince Rick that this reevaluation would help him, and it wasn't until his junior year that we began to make real progress. Thus, his first two years with us at the LSC were a continual, virtual tug-of-war about his need for intervention and ongoing, intensive academic support. Somewhere deep down he knew he needed it, but he did not suffer it gladly. Still, he came regularly, and always on time. This told me that we had reason to hope for his eventual success.

Look for the positives, progress is often very slow.

The first thing Rick and I had to come to terms with were his behavioral problems, which often accompany attentional disorders to some degree. I sensed that he did not have the ability to self-monitor his study behaviors, much less his cursing and mini-outbursts of anger in our sessions. Another tutor and I gave him a "grace" period to see if things got better as he became more comfortable with us, but his frustration and anger began to escalate because he lacked so little control over his impulses and thought patterns. We could make little progress until we resolved this to some degree, but Rick was not open to discussing it—he honestly did not see these things in himself. One day I decided to press on with tutoring when he was frustrated and wanted to leave; I "fed the flames," so to speak, to see if I could bring things to a head. Once he had displayed an actual temper tantrum, he was better able to see his behavior as we discussed it as objectively as possible afterward. Luckily, my intuition had been right—I sensed that we would continue to be stuck in the same patterns of interaction unless I could gently nudge him toward a clear display of behavior that would not be overridden by his severe distraction. When I did not judge him but merely noted what happened and explained what was appropriate behavior for him in a tutorial relationship, he seemed somewhat relieved. I gave him some "time out" in the room while I went to my desk to work quietly, telling him that we still had enough of our hour left to do some meaningful work; I reinforced that his outburst would not end our

Prioritize student needs for success and concentrate on the most critical first.

Beware of judging students.

session. In ten minutes, he was ready to resume work with me on his essay.

After he left, I reflected on what we had achieved: Rick had been about as "bad" as he could be with an authority figure, and he was not rejected, so trust was established. He learned that his temper *After meetings* would not excuse him from his work with me, and that the center *reflect on what* was a safe place to be if he wanted to be himself. Most of all, *was* however, he took his first real step on the lengthy, rough road of *accomplished.* learning just what his disability was all about and what he would need to do to accommodate.

Soon after, I convinced Rick to allow me to arrange accommodations with his professors for extended time exams in a quiet room and reasonable extensions on assignments, when needed. I kept reminding him of the need for a reevaluation, but he was not ready. I did, however, have enough information from his high school records to appropriately arrange for services under Section 504 regulations; still, our knowledge of the kinds and the extent of the problems he had was limited. He clearly did not want to have a documented disability, and rejecting further probing was an avoidance strategy that lent him added security for the time being. We continued doing the customary study strategies—having him keep detailed lists and calendars so he didn't forget to attend to responsibilities, having him work with tutors on reading and writing assignments, doing error analyses of exams to prepare for subsequent ones, and going over and over the basic principles of effective notetaking and study skills. The one constant we found was that with Rick there was little carryover to the next session, so continual reinforcement of past sessions was built into his tutorials.

Luckily, I was able to convince him to work with a personal counselor at the college's counseling center; these sessions helped *Work with* him somewhat to deal with his anger, frustration, insomnia, *other personnel* "hyper" feeling, anxiety, and lack of ability to monitor behaviors. *and encourage* This left us more time in tutorials to handle problems with course *students to take* work. In general, he was in need of a lot of intervention on a *advantage of* continual basis, as without this supervision, he would easily lose *services offered* focus and regress. We all experienced many "regressions" and *on campus.* "catch-ups" with him, not at all an unusual pattern in individuals with severe attentional disorders. Shortly before he graduated, he revealed to me that he believed he had never once finished any of *Monitor* his long reading assignments; he depended a lot on his lectures and *changes.* class notes to pull him through exams.

Finally, in his junior year, I was successful in convincing him to see a practitioner in the area for updated testing. The report confirmed a profound attentional disorder and suggested referral to a neurologist and psychiatrist to rule in or out other possible organic factors. His neurological exam was normal and, after that experience, he decided he didn't want to see any more doctors. It wasn't until months later that I was able to convince him to see a local psychiatrist who specialized in the diagnosis/treatment of adolescents and adults with ADD/ADHD. The results of Rick's formal diagnosis and treatment with medication were monitored by both of us with a lot of anticipation; ultimately, we were both pleased with the results.

Once the Ritalin prescribed for him took effect, I saw a different young man appear at my door one morning. He stood there, relaxed, leaning against the door jamb, a smile on his face, saying, "Hey—what's happening?" I called in the tutor who had been working closely with him, and we both sat down as he took his customary seat in my office. We watched him, then looked at each other in a bit of wonder—no significant leg jiggling, foot tapping, hand twitching, eye scanning, negativity, or disorganization of thought and conversation. He was better able to carry on a well-connected and comprehended conversation, and his usual wit and wry humor that always had a sarcastic edge to it was now more free-flowing and upbeat. Lest this spontaneously disappear as quickly as it seemed to appear, I packed him off to his tutorial session so he could get caught up on some work he had fallen behind in while adjusting to the medication. Afterward, he stopped at my door to ask if I thought the medication made that much difference. I told him that I thought it was making certain biochemical "adjustments" so he had better control of mental focus, but beyond that I could not say since we had been doing so much hard work for so long. He was uncomfortable with the thought that a drug would make that much difference, but when he ran out or forgot to take it, we would see a return of symptoms. Still, I believed, and made it clear to him, that all of the external structures and strategies that we had applied were finally "kicking in" in conjunction with the Ritalin, that it was all one continuous process. I think this made him feel better about taking the drug, but he was never entirely at ease with it.

There is no "quick fix" for a disability.

Rick needed only an extra summer school session his senior year to complete his degree requirements; we had told him that it might be a good idea to ease up on the credit load and take an extra semester or two, but he was determined to graduate as close to the rest of his class as possible. Until he finished, he continued to use our services, attend the counseling center, and consult with the psychiatrist as he continued the Ritalin. We watched his grades improved to a C+ overall and were pleased that his behavior start-

Disabilities and accommoda- tions are whole life issues.

ed to even out. He even began to articulate plans for his future, something he had been unable to attend to previously. One problem was that his aspirations were often incompatible with his "reality." He always had a great deal of trouble accepting his learning disorder and the limitations it would continue to place on him. Careers with the CIA and Secret Service were out of the question, and this frustrated him. He desperately wanted this "thing" he had to be school-related only; we spent many hours talking about how it was a whole life issue, but he never quite understood that. I realized that he would have to leave school and find that out for himself on the outside. Unfortunately, he did.

I spent a lot of time with Rick on the phone and in letters helping him with his major transition. He was living with family, holding down a menial job given his education and intelligence, he thought, and this bothered him. He wanted to be like his brother and sister, who were successful in careers and living on their own. He was very reluctant to continue with psychiatric help and, perhaps, medication; it was months of frustration and dissatisfaction before he sought further help. It seems to be helping some, but his severe attentional difficulties make it hard for him to handle a life completely on his own, for now anyway.

Educators constantly learn from each student and apply that knowledge to future students.

I believe, eventually, that Rick will find his niche in the greater world, one that will complement the positive aspects of his unique way of operating. He will also learn, with counseling and time, that he is the valuable and endearing person we all came to feel affection for. His boundless energy, persistence, and wry humor are qualities that got him through school, and they can get him through life, as well. If he can learn to accept that being different is not necessarily a bad thing, as we did in accepting him the way he was, he might even surprise us and make it in a demanding career. That is what I wish for him, and much more, for all that he taught me about acceptance, teaching, counseling, patience, friendship, and persistence—things that will help students he will never know. In this, perhaps, he will have found one of his greater successes.

Barry: A Case Study on Social Adjustment
by Jeanne L. Higbee

Five years ago a colleague knocked on my door on the first day of class and announced, "You're Barry's counselor. He's incredible! What a con artist! I just wanted to come and warn you about him." She proceeded to describe her encounter with Barry after their first class, "What a sob story. He told me he left his new checks in his parents' car and had no money to buy his books. Then he asked if he could use my automatic teller machine (ATM) card. Do you believe it?"

As liaison between our academic division and the campus Learning Disabilities (LD) Center, I immediately recognized Barry's name. Prior to the academic year I receive lists of self-identified disabled students from both the LD Center and the institution's Office of Disability Services. I then seek permission to share specific information regarding the nature of the student's disability with members of the faculty in order to provide appropriate academic accommodations.

Permission must be secured from the student before any information about his disability is shared.

I welcomed my colleague into my office and reviewed Barry's file, including a thorough profile and testing results from the LD Center. I explained that Barry has an organizational deficit in addition to a reading disability. He is very sincere and conscientious, and would never knowingly attempt to con anyone. Most likely he had never controlled his own finances before, and did not understand how ATM cards work. I assured the faculty member that I would speak with Barry.

I called Barry and asked him to meet with me regarding the potential need for notetakers and/or testing accommodations. At the end of our meeting I casually mentioned my interaction with Barry's professor. Barry had thought that if he used someone else's ATM card with his own code number, which he had memorized upon his parents' insistence, he could access money from his own account. At first my colleague was skeptical, and questioned my gullibility, but said she would give Barry the benefit of the doubt.

The history of the student provides insight into how the disability impacts learning.

The purpose of this subchapter is to provide an example of the social adjustment problems of some disabled students. Even faculty who have a thorough understanding of learning disabilities are frequently unaware of some of the inappropriate behavior patterns that accompany these learning deficits. In addition, students with acquired brain injuries and psychologically disabled students are two of the growing segments of the disabled student population at the college level. Some of these students become easily frustrated or anxious, and their behavior may reflect their emotionality. By law, the institution is not required to serve students who are disruptive, in other words, interfere with other students' opportunity to receive the full benefit of instruction. However, when possible, without infringing on the rights of other students, faculty are expected to accommodate these students.

Effective compensating strategies must be utilized so that other students are not impacted. Counseling support helps.

After responding to the initial crisis with Barry's instructor, I called the LD Center and set up a "staffing." All faculty members teaching Barry during his first term were invited, in addition to the

LD Center personnel who has tested him and those who would be providing such services as weekly counseling, arranging testing accommodations, and establishing tutoring schedules. At the staffing we reviewed Barry's assessment results, and then discussed implications for instruction. The faculty consistently reported Barry's behavior in the classroom as resistant, bordering on hostile. His attitude was establishing the tone in each of his classes. Barry frequently interrupted lectures with questions that challenged the authority of the teacher. Other students appeared to be frustrated and irritated by Barry's interference with the normal flow of the educational process. The faculty members were concerned that they would not be able to adequately cover the subject matter if they continued to divert class time to responding to Barry. They also resented the negative impact he had on the classroom environment. Individual interactions with Barry seemed more positive. He was perceived as pleasant, but manipulative.

The LD Center staff explained that Barry's disruptive behavior in class was a manifestation of his own sense of frustration. The solution to eliminating the negative behavior was to reduce Barry's anxiety regarding his ability to be competitive in a rigorous academic setting. There was no question that Barry was bright, even gifted in some subject areas. His disability impeded his performance, especially on written tests. Barry's inability to retain information and organize it logically resulted in his defensive demeanor. The LD Center staff provided a list of recommendations to enhance learning.

First, Barry was provided with a notetaker for each class. Then he could focus on what the professor was saying rather than how to organize the information on paper. It was agreed that Barry's exams would be administered orally at the LD Center. Each testing session would be taped for the instructor. Each teacher set up a weekly individual meeting with Barry to provide clarification and support. I received weekly progress reports and discussed them with Barry in our individual sessions. I also talked with him about his classroom behavior. He was to restrict his questions to only those absolutely necessary, and to wait until the end of class, if possible. The faculty members were encouraged to preview at the beginning of class, summarize at the end, and provide more handouts. Any behavioral problems were to be referred to me.

Often firm boundaries must be established when working with students.

Support by the teaching faculty leads to increasing self-confidence for the student.

As Barry became more comfortable at the university my contact with his teachers diminished. Before long Barry had earned the trust of the faculty member who had first knocked on my door, and was a daily visitor to her office, seeking special assistance in mastering the course material. By the end of the quarter she was serving as an ombudsperson on his behalf regarding the objective testing required to exit our program.

Last spring I chatted with Barry at an LD Center recognition reception. He was about to graduate with a Bachelor's degree of Education in Recreation and Leisure Studies and had established employment opportunities through his internship experience. Barry asked me to share this information with the faculty member he credited with his retention at the institution, my colleague. *Successful strategies lead to learning independence and these include social accommodations as well as those affecting academe.*

Barry's problems are not uncommon among disabled students. College personnel must be prepared to assist these students in adjusting socially as well as academically, and should be aware of the relationship between the cognitive and affective aspects of learning in order to address student needs.

Can We Talk?
by Nancy Poling

Perhaps I was in a more relaxed mood than usual; for as I documented my day's activities, I realized that most of my time with students had been spent in conversation. Diverging from our usual goal-directed activities, such as understanding the reading assignment or proofreading a paper, we had sat at the table discussing their concerns or interests. Robert, the visually impaired young man, interested in history, talked in great detail of a book he had read about the last emperor of China. Mike, a shy young man with a learning difference, wanted to wander from the communications assignment to discuss the ethics of a recent incident between NBC and General Motors. Paula, who also learns differently, was eager to get my opinion on free-will versus determinism, a topic being discussed in her philosophy class. *Professors should take time to review their interactions with students periodically.*

Contemplating my day I began to wonder about the interactive opportunities available to these students. Who do they discuss their ideas with? The image that came to me was one of social isolation.

This image seemed especially true of Paula. She is an African-American on a mainly white campus; an overweight woman among women who will destroy their health to stay thin; a commuter to a mainly residential campus; a student whose learning style is incompatible with a syllabus that requires essay tests and term papers.

For two years Paula had stopped by the learning center for occasional help, but it was not until she took Introduction to Philosophy, which required a weekly essay, that she began to make regular appointments with me. Gradually her history as a learner unfolded. Though the public school system had identified her as learning disabled and had placed her in special classes, no one had ever explained to her what her disability meant. She assumed it meant that she lacked intelligence.

Yet she quietly persisted in getting a college education, usually sitting in the back of the class, never contributing to discussion for fear her ideas would sound stupid. I picture Paula successfully trying to be invisible, all the while her head full of questions and observations.

Good teaching practices including verbal interactions among all students may be the key to actively involving the student with a disability in the learning environment.

Now, in the privacy of my office, she could discuss those wonderful ideas swirling in her head. As we worked on organizing the essays for philosophy, we took extra time to energetically discuss the issues the assignment raised. During the semester Paula discovered she could think; I rediscovered the value of dialogue as a teaching tool. Of course, Socrates saw its benefits a long time ago.

Dialogue is valuable in that it affirms students' intellect. Rather than search for right answers, partners in conversation assume that the other has thoughts to share. Also, as the teacher models a style of thinking, he/she exemplifies the value of intellectual growth and interaction throughout one's life.

Dialogue motivates students. After the discussion about China's last emperor, the history student used the topic in his speech class. The communications student chose the topic of ethics for a term paper. Paula has since started to view herself as a student, a real student.

Properly identifying learning strengths and using them can lead to the enjoyment of learning.

Next semester the head of the sociology department is allowing Paula to take an independent study with me. When I asked her what she thought about reading recent books on the history of the African-American family, her eyes lit up. When I said she wouldn't have to write a paper but that we would discuss the books, she expressed enthusiasm. There's little doubt in my mind that she'll be an eager student.

Often an accommodation is simply providing an opportunity.

Students who learn differently or who have physical disabilities may have limited opportunities for discussing their ideas and questions. The developmental educator can lessen social isolation by initiating discussion and by creating forums where education and social interaction converge.

Instructional Accommodations for Students Impacted by Social Behavior Disorders or Difficulties with Consistent Performance

supplementary text materials
signal-inappropriate behavior
notetaker or tape recorder
alternate testing location
discuss class behavior
frequent deadlines
weekly meetings
study schedule

Chapter 10
TEACHING STUDENTS WITH SPEECH AND LANGUAGE DIFFICULTIES

A student with a disability in speech or language may have difficulties in one or more of the following areas: pitch, loudness, articulation, syntax, phonology, or fluency. Classes requiring oral presentations and discussions may need to be adapted. Difficulties in speech may also lead to the need for accommodations related to grammar, spelling, and syntax in written work. Requirements in computer programming, mathematics, and a second language may also be affected. (Lissner, 1992)

Commonly Associated Disabilities

developmental language disorder
learning disability—semantics
deafness and aphasia
respiratory disorder
speech impairment
head trauma
stuttering

The establishment of good communication is the foundation of student success. Here is a list of questions to consider or discuss with the student who has a speech or language disability.

1. In what ways can I objectively evaluate the student's written work? (discount logical misspellings)
2. Does this student use a voice output computer or other speech generation technology? Is this something that will be integrated into a traditional classroom setting or is it needed only during specific situations?
3. What can I do to assist the student who uses American Sign Language (ASL) to practice standard English in nongraded situations and to interact meaningfully with other class members?
4. Do I need to allow alternate formats for oral presentations?

Hope and Help for Students with Severe Spelling Deficiencies
by Mildred R. Steele

The student with a disability can not be cured of the disability.

Traditional spelling procedures (e.g, memorization, mastering spelling rules, sounding out words), meet the needs of many students who want to improve their spelling abilities. However, these same techniques, in the hands of students with serious spelling deficiencies,[1] can be a disaster.

In the 1970s I became head of a new tutoring center in a four-year liberal arts college. We offered tutoring in many subject areas and also in reading, writing, and spelling. By the end of the first year, I noticed that our spelling program, which worked well with many students, was not effective with others.

The student's learning strengths must be part of the compensating strategy.

Why, I wondered, did some students work their way through our spelling program and then score virtually as low in the posttest as they had in the pretest? At first I rationalized that they might be students who hadn't applied themselves well, and probably I was right in some cases.

Most personnel who interact with the student will not be trained as a disabilities specialist.

From my reading and conversations with other faculty that first year, I began to suspect that learning disabilities might account for some of the difficulties of the students who made little spelling progress. However, I was not a learning disabilities specialist, and I had neither the staff, budget, nor mandate to set up a program to identify learning disabled students. The task of the tutoring center was to work with all students who wanted and/or needed help, and even in the early years our center was a success, measured by most standards of the time. One out of every three students on campus came to the center for tutoring each year, and most of them came voluntarily. Our student ratings were high, and we kept careful records that documented individual student progress. Nevertheless I was uneasy about the students whose learning needs we could not seem to accommodate.

Then one day in 1982 a freshman that I'll call "Jeff" came to the tutoring center for help in spelling. I knew that Jeff was a diligent student, and that he had a learning disability, diagnosed in his high school days. We gave him our spelling pretest, and it showed that he had spelling deficiencies in eleven out of fourteen spelling areas. Jeff was clearly a motivated student, so I started him out with our traditional spelling program that had worked with many students. Through it, he was to learn the rules that govern the spelling of each type of word and the chief exceptions. Jeff studied chapters 1, 3, 4, 6, and 7, which represented his first set of low areas, and was briefly tested over each chapter as he completed it.

The college provides learning support to the student and the student is comfortable in asking for help.

Then I gave him the first half of the posttest. Jeff's posttest scores indicated that, despite his diligence, he had made satisfactory improvement in only one area out of seven—minimal progress at best. It was obvious to us both that a program based on mastering and recalling spelling rules was not an answer to Jeff's learning needs.

The learning history of the student can help provide insight into the problem being faced.

At that point I recalled that a spelling kit had recently arrived on my desk. I had not yet tried it out, but I asked Jeff if he would be willing to try a new spelling technique that might be more helpful. What did he have to lose? He agreed, and I got out the tactile-kinesthetic kit (TKM).[2] Together we watched the filmstrip that explained and demonstrated the TKM technique. The procedure involved the repetitive use of a number of senses—visual, auditory, tactile, and kinesthetic—in learning to spell a word. We both practiced the technique with the filmstrip.

Feedback between the student and the learning skills specialist in the lab is provided through guided exploration.

In the kit, authors Mary Wortham and Betty Heinze explained the theory that underlies the technique, based on research by Drs. Grace Fernald, Elena Boder, and Howard Walton: Spelling methods that employ memorization involve three areas of the brain, four if reading is involved. Therefore students who learn readily through visual processing can expect success with any well-designed spelling program based on it. However students who need a multi-sensory approach are more likely to benefit from a tactile-kinesthetic program such as Wertham and Heinze's TKM, for it involves up to eleven areas of the brain.

Back in the tutoring center we identified ten words that gave Jeff trouble, and he went off to a library study room to work on them, using his newly-acquired spelling technique. When he came back about half an hour later, I tested him on the ten words and he spelled all of them correctly and asked for ten more. Within a few days, he had used the TKM technique on many of Brown and Pearsall's 336 core words that gave him trouble, and I gave him the second half of the posttest.

We were both a bit surprised but very pleased that Jeff achieved near-perfect scores this time on his posttest. I encouraged Jeff to continue to use the TKM technique not only on vocabulary words but on other key terms, such as his advisor's name and technical words he encountered in his studies.

I soon added the TKM spelling technique to our spelling options, working out procedures, preparing script word cards for Brown and Pearsall's core words, and training the tutoring staff. Before long our tutors were adept at working with students who used TKM, and most students who used the tutoring center were not aware that two spelling programs were in use.

Over the next eight years the TKM spelling program became a valuable resource at our tutoring center. Most students continued to use *Better Spelling* as before, but I estimate that at least 1,200 students learned to use the TKM technique during those years. Most who used it correctly and consistently showed as much improvement as Jeff did in his second posttest.

Spelling improvement was, of course, the bottom line. However, equally as important in my mind was the increase in self-esteem that we saw in these students who found that they could now spell much more confidently and competently.

Identifying and using successful learning strategies leads to increased self-confidence.

Though we relied on the two spelling programs at the tutoring center, we knew that neither was a panacea. There are too many variables beyond our control. Some students have learning or other problems far more complex than either a traditional or a multisensory spelling technique can address. Human nature being what it is, some students for any number of reasons simply go through the motions of any technique and fall by the wayside. Nevertheless the tactile-kinesthetic spelling program, over the years, enabled us to offer hope and help to Jeff and to many students with severe spelling deficiencies.

NOTES

1. This is a relative term, of course. In our tutoring center we ordinarily considered a student to have "serious spelling deficiencies" if most of his or her scores in our spelling pretest were at the fiftieth percentile or lower of all college students, that is, on or below the heavy horizontal line on the student's spelling chart. The percentiles had been established by James I. Brown and Thomas E. Pearsall in their research. The pretest we used was adapted from the diagnostic spelling test in *Better Spelling* by Brown and Pearsall (Lexington, MA: D. C. Heath and Company, 1978). Brown and Pearsall's test involves spelling 140 words of fourteen word types. In our tutoring center we rarely had time to

give such a lengthy test, so we used seventy of the Brown and Pearsall words for the pretest and the other seventy for a posttest, making sure that each test included equal numbers of words of the fourteen types. In addition, we ordinarily gave the posttest (on cassette tapes) in two parts in order to maximize student recall. In adapting Brown and Pearsall's test, we sacrificed some precision, to be sure, but the testing was satisfactory for our purposes and far less time consuming.

2. Mary H. Wortham and Betty L. Heinze, *Spelling Technique. A Tactile-Kinesthetic Method for Adults*. (Groveland, CA: Tutortapes, 1977). In brief the method is as follows: The person obtains a card with the word to be studied handwritten (NOT printed) in large script. 1. With arm and elbow on the table trace the word with finger pressure, feeling each movement. 2. Trace again, while pronouncing (not spelling) the word three or more times. 3. Finger-write the word on the table top while pronouncing it. 4. Using a pen or pencil, write the word on scratch paper while saying it, and check to make sure that each spelling is correct. 5. Repeat step 4 two more times.

Instructional Accommodations for Students Impacted by Speech and Language Difficulties

individual sessions by appointment
more writing, less talking
assistive technology
sign interpreter

Chapter 11
TEACHING STUDENTS WITH VISUAL IMPAIRMENTS OR BLINDNESS

A student with a visual impairment may have difficulty with visual acuity ranging from blindness to low vision, visual discrimination, or both; while a student experiencing problems with visual discrimination may find it difficult to separate the background from the foreground or to accurately follow printed information. (Lissner, 1992)

Commonly Associated Disabilities

learning disabilities—vision
head trauma
low vision
blindness

The establishment of good communication is the foundation of student success. Here is a list of questions to consider or discuss with the student who is visually impaired or blind.

1. Do I need to briefly review acceptable behavior toward a guide dog to class members?

2. Do I identify myself as I meet or greet the student? Is my tone of voice the same?
3. What appropriate teaching adjustments should I make?
4. What assistance can I provide the student who is taping lecture notes, using a note-taker, or using a Braille writer? What works well for the student and what does not?
5. Could a learning facilitator assist the student during classroom instruction or in a laboratory?
6. Do I verbalize what is written on the blackboard or overhead projector?
7. Do I encourage interaction of other class members with the student?
8. What testing formats are appropriate for the student?
9. Is assistive technology available to the student on campus? What is it and where is it?

Scotopic Sensitivity: Irlen Syndrome
by Judy Barnes

Johnna first came to me because she was having difficulty passing the required basic skills test of the Texas Academic Skills Program (TASP). Johnna is a friendly and attractive sophomore student at Tyler Junior College (TJC). She had easily passed the math section of the TASP test on her first attempt. On her second attempt, she passed the grammar/writing part; but she literally went to sleep during the reading section.

To learn more about Johnna's learning style and to identify possible problems, I questioned her extensively about her reading. She reported no vision or hearing problems. Her vision had been professionally checked within the last year. She said she had been taught phonics and felt she could read well except when it came to long passages. These she described as "BORING!" furthermore, she revealed that she had always had problems in school but was never tested for a learning disability and/or dyslexia. Her parents

The student had developed strategies.

had her privately tutored for several years, and she had developed strategies to compensate for her problems. For example, she had learned to scan for material needed in a reading assignment so she could get in and out of the printed page quickly. She stated that she had never read an entire book.

Testing is done by the appropriate professionals. It is separate from the teaching faculty. Some colleges provide this service to all students.

Because of her past history of academic struggles and the large variance in TASP scores, I decided to test her for a learning disability. Using the Wechsler Adult Intelligence Scale-Revised, I found that she was well above average in intelligence with definite strengths in verbal comprehension and math. I then used the Woodcock-Johnson Psycho/Educational Battery to assess achievement. Her math skills were well above average and were consistent with IQ. Johnna's English grammar and writing skills were lower than IQ, but not significantly. However, the reading score was low enough to meet eligibility criteria for a learning disability. Additional miscue analysis of reading revealed reversals, substitutions, and omissions that are frequently associated with dyslexia.

Since the testing established that Johnna had excellent intelligence and was literate, I recommended that she be enrolled in a developmental reading class that was designed for learning disabled students. This class is a cooperative effort between support services and developmental reading. Admission to the class is limited to students that have a documented learning disability. The textbook was developed locally for this class to emphasize college-level reading skills and to provide informative articles for learning disabled students. Some of the articles the students read are, "What is a Learning Disability?" "How Will My Learning Disability Effect My Education and Career?" and "What is Self Advocacy?" In my experience, learning disabled students have little understanding of their handicap and are very frustrated. This includes those who have been formally identified and have received special help for years. It seems that no one has explained learning disabilities or dyslexia to the students themselves. Thus they recognize they have academic problems and they label themselves "dumb." Therefore, the articles in the textbook are used to counsel the learning disabled, to build self-esteem, and to teach coping skills.

Eligibility criteria exists for student classification.

As I worked with Johnna through the summer, I was bothered by her comments of the material being boring and putting her to sleep. I noticed that she would read only a few minutes and then take a short break. This did not appear to be malingering but a way to cope with reading. I was puzzled as to why. Johnna confessed that after reading for fifteen to twenty minutes she would literally go to sleep as she did during the state TASP test. I wondered if she may have a form of light sensitivity that is found with some dyslexics (Scotopic Sensitivity/Irlen Syndrome—SSS). I had just finished being trained to screen for SSS, but I was still doubtful about its efficacy. It seemed too easy to be helpful. So I decided to experiment with Johnna. The screening indicated that she has this syndrome. The way she described what she sees when she reads is that the words on the page begin to move in a circle. The longer she reads the worse it becomes. If she really concentrated, the word she focused on would remain clear but all of the other words on the page swirl hypnotically around it.

Self-esteem is a catalyst in the development of academic coping skills.

Perceptual problems and visual problems are easily confused.

Helen Irlen, who developed this screening method, also found that pieces of colored plastic or overlays were helpful for some individuals. It is noted that this is a perceptual problem and not a visual problem. The current thinking is that the person is very sensitive to light bouncing from the page, which results in the visual distortions. The color overlays slow down the light waves and the distortion decreases. It is interesting that individuals prefer different colors so that no one color overlay helps everyone.

Guidance is given to identify the specific problem and how it impacts learning. Solutions are found through experimentation.

I proceeded to try to find whether or not a color or combination of colors would benefit Johnna. After trying several, she identified a combination that she felt was comfortable and made the print more readable. This did not totally stop the visual perceptual distortions, but it lessened them considerably. To test this, I repeated the Woodcock-Johnson Psycho/Educational Battery, Reading Comprehension Test. Using the overlays, her reading comprehension score increased from fifth to twelfth grade level. Again the overlays did not cure the dyslexia. Johnna is still dyslexic/learning disabled. But she now has a crutch that makes reading a "doable" endeavor.

Johnna now has a better understanding of her academic problems and frustrations. Her learning disability has been identified and she understands that she is an intelligent student who happens to have a handicap. She now has an explanation of why she has had such problems with classes that require extensive reading. She also knows how to ask for help and is aware of the type of help available at TJC—extended time on tests, oral testing, use of Kurtzweil Reading machine, notetaker in class, and so on. In addition, she knows to use the overlays when she reads to lessen the visual distortion on the printed page. With this she can read for longer periods of time and concentrate on comprehending rather than just identifying words. Again, Johnna's problems are not eliminated. However, she now has the understanding and resources to make reading college material possible. Her frustration has lessened and her college grades are steadily improving.

Tactile Learning for the Blind and Visually Impaired
by Kay Haralson

Success depends on effort by the student as well as accommodation by the instructor.

During my eighteen years of teaching mathematics, I have encountered students with many types of disabilities. I have had the opportunity to teach students with hearing impairments, visual impairments, learning disabilities, brain damage, personality disorders, and mobility impairments. To give credit where credit is due, most of these students adapted themselves to my teaching, rather than requiring major modifications on my part. I have adapted my classroom teaching by speaking distinctly so deaf students could read my lips, enlarging tests and lecture notes to enable visually impaired students to see the material, and allowing extra time on tests or giving oral tests for students with the need. In most cases, the accommodations I have made, and the efforts of the students to adjust have led to success in the course.

Last year my ability to communicate mathematics was challenged as never before. Allen, a student blind since birth, was enrolled in my Basic Arithmetic and Elementary Algebra classes. Allen attended a private high school in a rural Eastern Tennessee community and had attended a school for the blind for part of elementary school. He was enrolled at Austin Peay State University along with his sighted sister. Allen could not maneuver around campus without the aid of a guide and a cane. He was many times led to class by fellow students who happened to see him sitting outside waiting for class. Allen's ACT scores indicated that he had great ability in the reading and writing areas, but was very weak in mathematics. It became apparent quickly that Allen's poor mathematics skills was not due to lack of intelligence, but lack of exposure. He had been introduced to very little mathematics above the arithmetic level.

In his first semester, Allen succeeded quite well in Basic Arithmetic. I made a point of saying everything I wrote on the board and describing the work I was doing. I tried to avoid phrases such as "*Look* at this example," "*See* what happened to the inequality." Allen tape recorded the lecture during class and later transcribed the tape into class notes using his Brailler at home. A colleague also read the text into a tape recorder for him to play back and "read" the assignment. Quizzes were given as take-home assignments, which his sister read and scribed for him. Tests were read to him in a separate room, with myself or another instructor recording his work and answers. Rarely was the test shortened, because he generally could finish in a reasonable length of time. Allen's ability to remember long problems and "hold" the steps in his mind when working problems with multiple steps was phenomenal. In this course Allen did not require the use of his Brailler for tests or quizzes. Allen earned an A in the course and he and I were quite pleased.

Often when one sense is impaired others are heightened.

I looked forward to working with Allen again the next semester, but soon realized he was not going to be able to succeed in algebra without some major accommodations or teaching style modifications. I was very lucky to have another colleague to act as a learning facilitator in the classroom. She led me on a quest for learning as much as possible concerning ways to help Allen understand algebra. Calls were made to the National Federation of the Blind, and the American Printing House for the Blind—companies

Modifications of teaching styles are often necessary to provide the accommodation that is appropriate.

that specialized in providing learning aids to the blind—and a visit was made to the Nashville School for the Blind. It was during this visit that my eyes were opened. We watched as a sighted instructor at the school typed on a Brailler an equation we had written, and typed each of the subsequent steps in Braille. With amazement, I realized I did not have to know or be able to read Braille in order for him to use it. I only had to allow Allen to type an equation I read to him on his Brailler, then read back to me the steps he was executing. Trying this on the next test, I was astonished at the quickness with which he typed and read the problems in Braille, and the accuracy with which he worked them. Allen had also obtained a "talking scientific calculator," which aided him in complex calculations. Then came the chapter on graphing. How do you explain to a student who has never had sight, what a *plane* "looks" like, or a *point* or a *parabola*? How do you make yourself *stop* thinking and saying "visualize" and start thinking "conceptualize"? Even with my continued efforts to describe what I was graphing in detail, he just was not getting it. A description of something you have never "seen" is not very enlightening. Again, I worked with the learning facilitator to find ways of communicating graphical concepts to Allen. We ordered a raised line drawing kit, which enabled me to show examples of graphs on a special type of plastic paper, which crinkled when written on with a special stylus. Allen could then use his fingers to "feel" the point, line, or parabola, and conceptualize its location and direction on the graph. Now hearing "the line tilts to the left," or "the point is in Quadrant II," or "the parabola opens up" had meaning to him. However, he still could not "see" to graph on this paper himself. The learning

Explore the use of qualified aides in the classroom to assist the student.

facilitator devised a graphing board for tactile exploration to conceptualize beginning coordinate geometry. For the first time, I saw understanding on Allen's face. We met with Allen several times outside of class to demonstrate the graphing board and to allow him to practice with it. The learning facilitator also attended class with Allen on the days graphing was used and guided him through the examples on the board. It was agreed by all that a learning facilitator in class was as important to Allen's success as having a signer was for a deaf student. He was allowed to use the graphing board to graph problems on the tests as well. With the additional learning devices used, Allen was again successful in this course.

After the second semester at Austin Peay, Allen's family moved to Eastern Tennessee and he left our university. Although teaching class next semester without Allen was easier for me, his presence in the class was missed. The students who had been in class with

Allen for two semesters had begun to realize how lucky they were to be able to "see" the work being presented and to appreciate the ability to quickly work through problems with paper and pencil. They developed patience with their fellow students and admiration for Allen for setting his goals on a college education. As for myself, I learned even more. I learned to always keep looking for that "special" way of communicating with a student and to never underestimate what determination and perseverance can accomplish. Through my teaching experiences with Allen, I discovered that to find the right method for teaching special students, you must know where to look and who to ask.

As more and more students with physical, psychological, or learning disabilities are admitted to colleges and universities across the nation, schools must set their goals on making a college education equally accessible to all. Universities must also accept the responsibility for providing the support system needed by these students and educating faculty members on the appropriate ways in which accommodations can be provided.

Working with Students with Visual Disabilities
by Carla Moldavan

My teaching experience has afforded me the opportunity to work with three students who were unable to see information written on a blackboard, on handouts, or in the textbook. Because my students had once had normal vision, working with them required fewer modifications than would have been necessary when working with a student who had been blind since birth. Nevertheless, it did require extra time, but that extra time provided me with the opportunity to learn from my students.

The first student, Fred, was blinded as a result of his service during the Vietnam War. Fred had a very supportive wife who helped him get to and around campus. Fred was able to succeed in my liberal arts math course by taping class sessions and receiving generous help in the math lab. At that time another instructor and I constituted the math lab staff, so I worked individually with Fred for extended periods. At times I would take Fred's hand to draw what I was describing in order to help him visualize. During class time I had to remember to explain everything slowly and clearly, always providing an oral presentation for material that was written on the board or asked about from the text.

Family support systems are often overlooked but have influence.

Teaching adjustments will often include the involvement of other senses.

Though my experiences with Fred were almost twenty years ago, I vividly remember Fred describing to me how he had astounded someone with whom he was riding in a car one day. He predicted when it was time to turn on a road, based on his discrimination of the different sound the car made when going across a bridge. Fred gave me this illustration to point out that many times people operate on the misconception that because a person's sight is impaired one must speak more loudly to make sure the person hears. The person's other senses may in fact be heightened when sight is diminished.

On the other hand, as the Coordinator of Disabled Student Support Services at Kennesaw State College (KSC) pointed out in a presentation to my freshman orientation class, if a person does have a hearing impairment in which messages are not heard clearly, the common practice of "speaking up" causes them merely to hear the muddled message more loudly. During that presentation, my

Investigate the availability of adaptive equipment.

class and I were made aware of the adaptive equipment available to students with disabilities. KSC happens to be one of the few schools in the country with the Dragon Dictate voice-recognition computer systems for individuals who cannot operate a standard keyboard.

Another system, Accent, provides voice output of the contents of the screen. WIZKEY provides word prediction capabilities, reducing the number of keystrokes needed by individuals who have difficulty using a standard keyboard. The institution has a Braille typewriter and a Telephone Device for the Deaf (TDD).

Enlargements with a computer or copy machine can be helpful.

For my most recent visually impaired student, Marshall, the resources most helpful were Zoomtext and the IBM Toolkit. Zoomtext and VISTA enlarge the contents of the computer screen. The IBM Toolkit provides the same capabilities as the TI-81 graphing calculator required in the algebra courses.

Marshall sees well enough to traverse campus unaided but cannot see a graphing calculator or textual material without magnification. I found that I could prepare my handouts and tests for Marshall by taking the disks on which they were prepared using WordPerfect and having the secretary print them on her printer using giant print. We brought the computer with IBM Toolkit to class for Marshall as well as had it available outside of class.

Communication within the university system is important.

Before each quarter begins the Coordinator of Disabled Student Support Services at KSC sends the student's instructors information on any student who has identified himself/herself as having a disability. The instructor is informed of the nature of the disability and the accommodations needed.

The years between my first two visually impaired students and the latest one have brought the provision of individual tutors who can even come to the class with the student and help take notes. The math lab provides further help and is staffed by student assistants. My college algebra class that Marshall attended was blessed to have several students who had already been with me through two quarters of developmental studies mathematics. Some of these highly motivated nontraditional students formed a study group that included Marshall. The outcome in grades for all three of my visually impaired students was the same—each earned a B. I know that Fred later transferred to a four-year institution and I conferred with a math instructor there regarding his math placement. Marshall is still on campus, enjoying his studies and doing well both personally and academically.

In summary, I would recommend to an instructor that he/she inquire as to what services are available to the disabled student through the institution. Rich surprises may be in store for you! Even if not, the main ingredient for success with a student with disabilities is patience, time, and a willingness to learn. And finally, as you remember to unravel the learning hierarchy to make sure all the prerequisites are present, also remember to state orally everything that takes place, doing so slowly and clearly, but not too loudly!

Inquire about services that are available on campus.

Unravel the learning hierarchy.

Educating the Visually Impaired
by Lynn Skaggs

Eric was a visually impaired incoming freshman in the fall semester. Because he had attended public schools in a remote small country town, Eric had limited knowledge of Braille and had had to rely on tutors and special education instructors in high school. So it was that I, as a reading instructor and tutor, came to know Eric.

Visual impairment is a dysfunction of the eye or the optic nerve that prevents an individual from seeing normally. The definition became very well known to me over the course of three years, as I guided Eric to an Associate of Arts degree. Eric had had visual impairment from birth. He was legally blind but preferred to be called visually impaired because he could see shapes and shadows. An individual is legally blind when central vision acuity is less than 10/200 in the better eye after best correction. Eric had roving eyes because he had never focused on things as sighted people do and the muscles were untrained. He was of average to above average intelligence and was otherwise physically normal.

The specific strategies that were used with Eric began the day that his advisor introduced us and requested help in our Academic Enrichment Center.

First, Eric and I set up a study schedule when we would meet to work together. He then talked to his instructors and informed them

Set up a
schedule
together.
Interact with
others to pool
knowledge.

The student
should check on
the availability
of adaptive
texts.

On occasion,
requirements
can be modified
or waived.

of his disability and limitations. For the most part all the faculty were supportive and understanding. On occasion, it was necessary for me to talk with some on a one-to-one basis about specific questions or concerns about getting homework or a test completed.

Eric was able to order about half of his texts from the Library of Congress. These books he would listen to in his dorm room during free or evening hours.

For the books that were not immediately available, we met in my office/classroom during the early afternoons, four days a week.

1. We used a normal classroom with regular light fixtures.
2. We sat at a round table with our chairs about three feet apart with the chairs slightly facing each other. We used the table to hold books, paper, and pencil for me and a recorder for the blind for him. He used the recorder about 30% of the time, preferring to rely on memory.
3. I read in a normal reading tone and pace.
4. We worked approximately two hours at a stretch.
5. Written work was accomplished within the same framework with Eric speaking and my taking notes and then writing them up. For long assignments, I gave the final draft to a typist and Eric paid her by the page.
6. Tests were hand delivered to the room, read aloud to Eric, marked and hand delivered back to the instructors.
7. Math instruction was done on a chalkboard by the math tutor on an individual basis.
8. The computer requirement was waived in Eric's case.
9. Other than the above two, Eric did all the work with me to complete his Associate of Arts in six semesters.

Eric was but one of many students who was assisted by our Academic Enrichment Center, as we customize study schedules and tutors to accommodate individual needs. In Eric's case, due to his specific daily needs, he spent more time with us than most other students. However, it was his persistence and desire to learn and my commitment to help him that resulted in his meeting his ultimate goal, graduation. Educating this visually impaired student has been one of our most memorable achievements and an important impetus for meeting the needs of our future students.

Instructional Accommodations for Students
Impacted by Visual Impairments or Blindness

more speaking and listening
notetaker or tape recorder
alternate testing location
less reading and writing
alternate testing format
learning facilitator
seating location
extended time
taped texts
reader
scribe

Chapter 12
FORMING A COALITION TO PROMOTE STUDENT GROWTH AND SUCCESS

Accommodating a disability—having a disability—is a whole life issue; it is not just related to the world of academe. Postsecondary institutions and their educators have the responsibility to accommodate students with disabilities and it must be student centered. Opportunities for the student to explore and investigate must be provided, keeping in mind that the student with disabilities may need guided exploration to find strengths that can be maximized while minimizing weaknesses and limitations. The ultimate goal of any institution of higher learning is to provide experiences that build self-confidence in the student. The subchapters in this book show clearly that high-priced technology and huge budgets are not the most important need for student success and a comprehensive network of services provide a catalyst to learning for all students. The following subchapter clearly summarizes the important give-and-take shown by the contributing authors and their students at their respective institutions.

Teaching Strategies and Accommodations for Students with Disabilities
by Wanda Baer

Over the years as I have worked with students, tutors, and faculty to develop ways to facilitate learning, I have come to believe that most individuals can learn, given adequate time and the use of appropriate teaching style and strategies. Individuals may have limits to their learning but many times these limits are self-imposed or societal. It has also been my experience that in the concentration on subject content learning, although very necessary, we have failed to help students "learn how to learn." This is often reflected in our inability to reach students who are unable to respond to the usual teaching methods because they have disabilities, physical, emotional, or learning. Although there may be a perception by some that in accommodating individual needs, providing alternatives or options, we are giving special treatment, this is not valid. It is more leveling of the playing field so everyone has an equal opportunity for learning. Teachers have found that by adapting teaching methods and strategies to meet the special needs of some students, all students can benefit. Therefore, my comments and suggestions are useful for all students, but very importantly, for those who have some form of disability.

Successful students must develop effective study strategies and habits. The admonition to study harder to succeed is difficult for students who have not developed an effective reading system, do not understand the importance of good notes, do not know how to organize their study time, or do not know how to take tests. Study strategies need to be taught along with compensating techniques for those who have a disability.

Motivation is another important factor in learning, and in learning for the sake of learning is not motivating for most students. Colleges develop curricula to meet the criteria of the disciplines and accreditation, but also for the working world. Students do not always recognize the significance of the relationship of subjects to that objective so have little interest to learn. Once they identify the why and the way they can use the information, there is more motivation.

Students are often not aware of their particular learning style so they do not know how to capitalize on their strengths or how to develop their weaker areas. Students who have some kind of disability are especially vulnerable in this area since they have fewer strengths to draw upon. It is important to provide students this framework for "learning how to learn," which is not just during their college days but for a lifetime.

Part of the orientation of students for college, especially students with disabilities, should be an empowering one: getting students to take control and responsibility for their own learning. To work toward that objective, students should be given a learning styles inventory and assessment of their knowledge and use of study strategies. There are numerous excellent instruments available. However, just giving the information is not enough. Students need to know how to use the information and how to transfer it from one discipline to another to be successful. This needs to be reinforced all through their academic days.

Students who have disabilities are often provided extra support through tutoring in high school. It is unfortunate that sometimes the focus there is on memorizing content to get through the class rather than on developing techniques or strategies for understanding the subject and using the information. Tutoring is of great value but it should be directed toward helping the student be independent so that he/she can be successful in the work world.

There is no doubt in these times that faculty experience a great deal of frustration over how to facilitate student success, especially those with special needs. There are no easy solutions, no pat answers. However, some of the following suggestions have been tried with success:

- The most successful teachers are those who have a high degree of knowledge of the discipline but also a great deal of enthusiasm for the subject—a joy of teaching.
- Faculty must be aware of the learning styles and the ways to capitalize on them in presenting content. Utilize the learning cycle: Why, What, How, What if, to facilitate classroom presentations, projects, homework. This includes an understanding of learning modalities: visual, auditory, kinesthetic.
- Faculty must be aware of personal learning style. Too often we teach, tutor, and train in the same manner as our personal learning style, which may not be compatible with that of many of our students.
- The students also need a validation of their learning preferences. Faculty need to affirm value of individual differences. There is no one right way of learning. Call attention to preferences in class presentations, activities, and so on, reinforcing information in the classroom to increase student awareness of the learning process.
- Faculty must look at course objectives and the many different ways they can be achieved to meet diversity. Students must be given options to meet those objectives.
- Faculty must promote collaborative learning to utilize each student's strength.
- Dyads are helpful for students in problem-solving situations. Students build effective learning strategies and techniques through their experiences so faculty must create opportunities for students to demonstrate their different approaches to learning, problem-solving, and so on. There is no one right way.
- Share your own processes. Too often faculty demonstrate procedures but not their own processes for selecting the steps or making choices.
- Provide an outline (on the board or handout) for each lecture.
- Use Bloom's Taxonomy in framing higher level questions for class discussion so that students develop critical thinking skills.
- Class discussions are valuable for auditory students and those with visual difficulties.

•When possible, provide untimed tests. The objective of testing should be to find out what students have learned not how rapidly their thinking processes work.

Colleges and universities who are committed to providing the best environment for all students can provide faculty workshops using simulation exercises to create a better understanding of the difficulties experienced by students with disabilities. There are many effective strategies to help students overcome a barrier to learning. But every student's need is different. Sometimes, the best action is to ask the student, "What works best?"

It is important that students accept responsibility for their own learning, but teachers must also accept responsibility for providing an environment that encourages learning, using a variety of teaching strategies with multisensory presentations to facilitate and enhance learning. Teaching and learning are on the same side of the coin, not on opposite sides.

As human beings, we are all learners.

As learners, some of us will learn in similar ways.

As individuals, each of us will learn in a different way.

When we can recognize, affirm, and celebrate those differences

We are all empowered for learning.

BIBLIOGRAPHY

Claxton, Charles S. & Murrell, P. (1987). "Learning Styles." *Higher Education Reports*. Ashe-Eric 4. 40-77.

Conner, James E. (1982). "Half a Mind is a Terrible Thing to Waste." *For Adults Only*. 15(1), Fall. North Carolina Department of Community Colleges.

Cornett, Claudia. (1983). "What You Should Know about Teaching and Learning Styles." Fastback, 191. The Delta Kappa Educational Foundation.

Dunn, Rita S. & Dunn, K. (1979). "Learning Styles/Teaching Styles: Should They. . . Can They Be Matched?" *Educational Leadership*, January, 238-244.

Golay, Keith. (1982). *Learning Patterns & Temperament Styles*. Fullerton, CA: Manas-Systems.

Guild, Pat Burke. (1985). *Marching to Different Drummers*. Alexandria, VA: Association for Supervision and Curriculum Development.

Kolb, David. (1986). *User's Guide for the Learning Style Inventory*. Boston: McBer and Company.

Leflar, Susan Morris. (1983) "The 4Mat System: An Interview with Bernice McCarthy." *Journal of Developmental & Remedial Education*. 6(2), 14-16, 29.

McCarthy, Bernice. (1985). "What 4Mat Training Teaches Us about Staff Development." *Educational Leadership*. April, 61-68.

Pintrick, Paul. (1989). "Student Learning and College Teaching", "The Dynamic Interplay of Student Motivation and Cognition in the College Classroom", "A Process Oriented View of Student Motivation and Cognition". *Advances in Motivation and Achievement*. M. Moehr, C. Ames (ed.) Vol 6, C1989 JAI, 117-160.

Stice, James E. (1987). "Improve Student Learning." *Engineering Education*. February, 77(5), 291-296.

Svinicki, Marilla D. "The Kolb Model Modified for Classroom Activities." *College Teaching*. 35(4).

The subchapters also show the personal side to teaching and learning. Successful colleges and universities are directly the result of good teachers making a difference student by student; this is achieved with the support of administrative units providing opportunities for all students working toward excellence. These networks of professionals represent a coalition that exists for the student at the colleges and universities represented by the contributing authors and at any other institution of higher learning. The coalition is student centered, and the three components that radiate to, from, and around the student are the Office of Disability Support Services (DSS), a center promoting academic achievement (learning center) and the teaching faculty.

COALITION MODEL FOR STUDENT SUCCESS

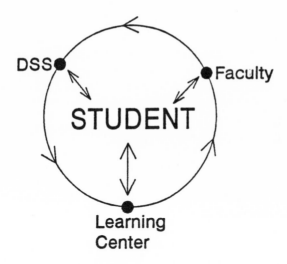

THE STUDENT

The responsibility of the student is to identify himself to the teacher when learning assistance is needed. The student actively seeks his best mode of learning and how to use it to his advantage. The student is committed to making sure that the following three components are working together with him.

THE OFFICE OF DISABILITY SUPPORT SERVICES (DSS)

The responsibilities of this office are to provide the foundation and structure for students with a disability and the university community as well as to serve as a liaison between these components. This office is the official record keeper for the students—all academic and medical records must be kept by this office. Also in place should be written guidelines on the determination of a disability and the need for accommodation as well as what is to be considered appropriate accommodation.

This office is often the student's first contact with the institution. It is the responsibility of DSS to provide students with the opportunity to set up meetings. The subchapter authors suggest that professionals in this office meet with students individually and provide opportunities for roundtable discussions for students with similar disabilities. Some institutions have successfully implemented these on a monthly basis, with the dates for these meetings scheduled at the beginning of the semester/quarter and entered into the student's personal calendar. When meeting with the student individually, it is this office's responsibility to help students set both short-term and long-term goals, as well as chart progress toward those goals and modify as necessary.

This office serves as a liaison between the student and all university services—from dormitories, to dining facilities, to the classroom. As the student gains more confidence in his abilities to achieve his educational goals, DSS will interact less and less with the student. The subchapter authors also suggest that the students who have been at the institution the longest serve as mentors and group leaders for those students who are new to the institution. Although this office does intervene and advocate for the student, this role should lessen as the student becomes more self-sufficient and ready to enter the job market.

DSS should also serve as a liaison with school officials involved with school policy. Certain situations require case-by-case decisions and effective committees must be in place to plan for situations that may arise. For example, a student who is deaf may request that American Sign Language (ASL) be a substitution for a foreign language requirement. These committees should represent a cross-section of the university population.

This office is also responsible for instructing and providing aid to faculty in accommodating students with disabilities. Professionals in DSS should be a resource for instructors trying to accommodate individual students. This can be done by meeting with faculty individually or in groups, and should be done on a continuing basis.

THE LEARNING CENTER

The responsibility of the learning center is to promote academic achievement by the student. Just telling a student what to do is not enough. Students need the opportunity to experiment, with trained guidance, to find what adaptations and accommodations best meet their learning style and academic/life needs. This center is where students can learn about learning and search for answers to the following two questions: 1. What are my learning strengths? and 2. How does my disability impact my learning? This center is the place where students go to investigate learning under the guidance of skills analysts, which are separate from academic content tutors. Study skills strategies need to be taught along with compensating techniques, from simple strategies like notecards to experimentation with different colored overlays, pens, paper, and lighting. Ideally, assistive technology should be available to the student at or near this center. Computers, graphing calculators, video tapes and tape recorders should all be available for student use; as well as personnel trained in the use of technology. It is here, also, that testing facilities are available for those students who need testing accommodations.

Tutors should be trained as skills analysts and be available to help students investigate their individual learning strengths and preferences. It has been suggested that upper level students in the fields of education and special education be used.

The development of critical thinking skills based on Bloom's Taxonomy can be utilized. Students should practice framing questions for a particular subject using Bloom's Taxonomy and working up the cognitive ladder guided by a skills analyst. The learning center is a resource that should be available to all students and not just to those with disabilities. The facilities are also available to faculty members, and personnel should present workshops to faculty on the specific resources at the center.

THE FACULTY

The faculty comprises educators accepting the responsibility for providing an environment that encourages learning, using a variety of multisensory teaching strategies to facilitate and enhance learning. Generally, the syllabus is the first contact a student has with a faculty member and it should clearly state the policies and requirements for a course, including a statement that encourages students with disabilities to make contact with the instructor as soon as possible. Once the student self-discloses, the instructor is responsible for discussing and providing reasonable accommodations. Instructors should implement different modalities of presentation into their classroom, being careful not to impose their learning styles on their students. Instructors should say out loud everything that is written on the board as well as provide simple, written instructions in addition to oral ones. They should also preview at the beginning of each class and summarize at the end. Outlines should be provided on the board, overhead, or in a handout for lectures, with charts and diagrams provided as necessary. Faculty who utilize Bloom's Taxonomy are aware of how students learn, how they think, and how they develop critical thinking skills. Faculty members should look at their course objectives and consider different ways they can be achieved to meet diversity. Students should be provided with *options* to meet the stated objectives, which include collaborative learning to maximize student strengths.

As the above coalition strengthens at each college and university, so too will access for higher education for all.

Appendix A
KEY FEDERAL LEGISLATION

THE REHABILITATION ACT OF 1973

Title V of the Rehabilitation Act of 1973 is considered the first federal civil rights legislation for persons with disabilities. Title V addressed nondiscriminatory hiring practices in federal agencies (Section 501); established the Architectural and Transportation Barriers Compliance Board (Section 502); requires affirmative action clauses for employment of qualified individuals with disabilities in the contracts of prime federal contractors bidding on jobs in excess of $2,500 (Section 503); requires nondiscrimination in employment and the provision of services by all programs receiving federal funding (Section 504); establishes remedies for discrimination and assigns regulatory responsibilities for enforcement (Sections 505–507).

This landmark legislation is still in force and served as a foundation for the Americans with Disabilities Act (ADA). A principal difference between the ADA and its predecessor is coverage. The Rehabilitation Act covers the recipients of federal funds, the ADA covers private entities, state and local governments in addition to recipients of federal funding. In addition to extending civil rights protection for individuals with disabilities, the enactment of the ADA has raised both public awareness and the awareness of individuals with disabilities of their rights.

THE AMERICANS WITH DISABILITIES ACT

The ADA is divided into five titles. Title I covers nondiscrimination in private sector employment. Currently, employers with twenty-five or more employees are covered; on July 26, 1994, employers with fifteen or more employees were covered. This title requires the employers not to discriminate on the basis of disability in the recruitment, hiring, retention, or promotion of qualified employees with disabilities. "Qualified" is judged on the basis of ability to successfully perform the essential job functions either with or without reasonable accommodations. Title II requires that public transportation, state and local government facilities, and programs be made accessible to individuals with disabilities. Title III requires that public accommodations (the programs, goods, and services provided to the public by either private or public entities such as malls, restaurants, and theaters) be made accessible. Title IV requires that telecommunication services be made accessible to persons with disabilities affecting hearing and speech. Title V contains miscellaneous provisions relating to the previous four Titles (e.g., exemptions for historic sites), remedies, and regulatory jurisdiction.

GENERAL REQUIREMENTS UNDER THE ADA
- No exclusion on the basis of disability.
- Notice of nondiscrimination and availability of accommodations.
- No discrimination through eligibility criteria.
- Modification in policies, practices, and procedures to ensure nondiscrimination and accessibility.
- Examinations and courses must be accessible.
- General services and programs must be accessible.
- Participation in the most integrated setting.
- Surcharges to cover the costs of accessibility may not be imposed solely on persons with disabilities.
- No discrimination through contract.
- Appointment of a compliance officer.
- Establish grievance procedure.

GENERAL TREATMENT OF STUDENTS UNDER SUBPART E, SECTION 504 OF THE REHABILITATION ACT
- Notice of nondiscrimination and availability of accommodations.
- Institution may not exclude qualified students with disabilities from any course, course of study, or other sponsored activity.
- Programs or activities not wholly operated by the institution but used in conjunction with institutionally sponsored programs must provide an equal opportunity for participation by qualified students with disabilities.
- All programs (curricular and cocurricular) must be accessible when viewed as a whole.
- Programs and services must be operated to allow participation by students with disabilities in the most integrated setting possible.
- Appointment of a compliance officer.
- Establish grievance procedures.

SPECIFIC REQUIREMENTS UNDER SECTION 504

Admissions and Recruitment
- The institution may not use any test or criterion for admission that has a disproportionate, adverse effect on individuals with disabilities.
- Admission and recruitment information must be available in accessible formats.
- Admission and recruitment activities must be held in accessible locations.
- Quotas for admissions of students with disabilities are prohibited.
- Preadmission inquiries concerning disabilities are prohibited.

Academic Adjustment
- Institutions must make modifications to academic requirements as necessary to ensure that such requirements do not discriminate or exclude students on the basis of disability.
- Evaluations of student performance, including course examinations, must be provided with appropriate modifications to ensure that the evaluation represents a student's achievement rather than reflecting the impact of a student's disability.
- Institutions are responsible for ensuring that students with disabilities are not denied access to the benefits of any sponsored program or activity because of the absence of auxiliary aids or services.

Physical Education and Athletics
- Institutions must offer equal opportunities for participation in physical education courses, intercollegiate, or intramural athletics to students with disabilities.

Housing
- An institution that provides housing to its students must provide comparable, convenient, and accessible housing to students with disabilities at the same cost as to others.

Financial Employment Assistance to Students
- Institutions may not limit eligibility for or provide less financial aid to students on the basis of disability.
- Institutions are prohibited from assisting any outside agency, organization or person in providing employment opportunities to its students if stated opportunities are not made available to all students, regardless of the existence of a disability.

Counseling Services
- Counseling services, including personal, academic, and career counseling must be provided without discrimination on the basis of disability.

Social Organizations
- An institution that provides significant assistance to fraternities, sororities, or similar organizations shall assure themselves that the membership practices nondiscrimination on the basis of a disability and that the activities of such organizations do not deny participation on the basis of disability.

The Relationship of the ADA to Section 504
The ADA does not replace Section 504 of the Rehabilitation Act. Where the jurisdiction and standard of access of the two acts overlap, the Department of Justice and the Department of Education's Office of Civil Rights have agreed that complaints will be evaluated and pursued under Section 504 regulations and case law. Where the ADA calls for a higher standard of access, complaints will be pursued by the Department of Justice under the ADA.

The Relationship of Federal to State Legislation
The ADA and Section 504 establish minimum accessibility and nondiscrimination guidelines. Both acts defer to any state or local legislation that requires a higher standard.

Appendix B
ACCOMMODATION DECISION MAKING PROCESS: IS THE STUDENT QUALIFIED?

I. Determine eligibility for accommodation.
    A. Can the student verify the disability (based on 504 definition) by observation or documentation?
       1. Not verified; the student is not entitled to accommodation but may pursue an appeal.
       2. Verified; go on to Step III.
II. Identify the academic and technical standards.
    A. For admissions.
    B. For course/program completion.
    C. For co-curricular program or service.
III. Is the student otherwise qualified?
    A. Can they meet academic and technical standards with accommodations or auxiliary aids?
       1. If no,
          a. Does the requirement or course represent an essential aspect of the student's program?
             i. If yes, the student is not otherwise qualified and not entitled to accommodation but may appeal.

        ii.If no, the course or requirement must be waived or substituted.
     2. If yes, student is otherwise qualified and must be accommodated.
     Go on to Step IV.
IV. Identify the accommodation options.
    A. Is there more than one possible accommodation?
       1. If yes, select an option based on the criteria below. Then go to Step V.
         a. Provides an equal educational opportunity.
         b. Allows the most integrated experience possible.
         c. Can be implemented in a timely fashion.
         d. Cost considerations.
       2. If no, then go to Step V with one accommodation.
V. Is the accommodation acceptable to the student?
    A. If yes, implement accommodation.
    B. If no, the student may pursue an appeal.

GUIDELINES FOR ACCOMMODATION DECISION MAKING

In reading the following guidelines, keep in mind that the purpose of providing accommodations is to allow students to meet established standards and to have an equal opportunity to benefit from services and programs.

1. Students must be informed of how to make a request for accommodation.
2. Students should both initiate the request and participate in the search for potentially reasonable accommodations.
3. Students may be required to provide appropriate documentation (medical evaluations, psycho-educational evaluations, and so forth) to support their request and assist in the process of identifying potential accommodation.
4. Accommodation decisions must be made on a case-by-case basis. While procedural guidelines should exist, there should be no formulas (disability X = accommodation Y) or statements that requests will not be considered for a particular requirement, program, or service.
5. The institution may establish standards that are fundamental or essential to a course, degree, program, or service. Such standards must be defined in meaningful ways that relate to the purpose of the course, service, or program in question. These standards are not subject to accommodation. Methods of evaluation and delivery are subject to accommodation.
6. The search for alternative methods of evaluation and delivery to accommodate a student should be conscientiously carried out, and include an exploration of new approaches or devices beyond traditional academic practice, and be documented. It is expected that the search will include input from appropriate professionals and state and federal resources in determining possible methods of accommodation.
7. When more than one equally effective method of accommodation exists, the institution may choose among them. Considerations in determining if accommodations are equally effective include the level of integration versus segregation and the level of potentially negative attention the method may attract for the student.

Denial of a request must be based on one of the following reasons:

1. There is no disability to accommodate.
2. The disability does not disproportionately impact the requirement, delivery system, or evaluation method in question.
3. The unique characteristics of the delivery system or evaluation method in question are integrally bound to a fundamental requirement and cannot be altered without a

substantial modification of an essential standard.
4. The accommodation in question would pose an undue hardship on the institution when its full financial resources are taken into account.
5. Due to the impact of the disability the student poses a real danger to self or others even in the presence of accommodations.

Appendix C
RIGHTS AND RESPONSIBILITIES

THE RIGHTS AND RESPONSIBILITIES OF _____
COLLEGE/UNIVERSITY

_____ College/University recognizes that its basic responsibility is to identify and maintain the academic and technical standards that are fundamental to providing quality academic programs while insuring the rights of students with disabilities. To meet these obligations, _____ College/University:

has the responsibility to inform its applicants and students about the availability and the range of accommodations.

has the responsibility to evaluate applicants based solely on their abilities. If an evaluation method or the criteria have a disproportionately adverse effect on an applicant with a disability, the college will seek reasonable alternatives.

has the responsibility to insure that all of its programs (not necessarily all physical facilities) are accessible.

has the responsibility to make reasonable adjustments in the delivery, instructional method, and evaluation system for a course when these have a disproportionately adverse impact on a disability.

has the responsibility to adjust, substitute, or waive any requirement/course that has a disproportionately adverse impact on a disability and is not fundamental to the student's academic program.

has the right to identify and establish the abilities, skills, and knowledge necessary for success in its programs and to evaluate applicants on this basis.

and its faculty have the right to identify and establish the abilities, skills, and knowledge that are fundamental to their academic programs/courses and to evaluate each student's performance on this basis. These fundamental program/course goals are not subject to accommodation.

has the right to request and review documentation that supports requests for accommodation. Based on this review, the college/university has the right to refuse an unsupported request.

and its faculty have a right to select among equally effective methods of accommodating a student with a disability.

has the right to refuse an accommodation based on undue hardship.

THE RIGHTS AND RESPONSIBILITIES OF STUDENTS WITH DISABILITIES

A student with a disability has the right to an equal opportunity to participate in and benefit from programs offered at _____ College/University. To insure this right, students with disabilities at _____ College/University:

have a responsibility to identify themselves as needing accommodation in a timely fashion. When the disability is not obvious, the student must provide documentation from an appropriate professional.

have a responsibility to demonstrate or document how their disability affects a particular delivery system, instructional method, or evaluation criteria when requesting accommodation.

have a responsibility to actively participate in the search for accommodations and auxiliary aids. This responsibility extends to working with the institution to seek financial assistance from government agencies and private sources.

have the same obligation as any student to meet and maintain the institution's fundamental academic and technical standards.

have a right to be evaluated based on their ability, not their disability. If their disability disproportionately affects the outcome of an evaluation method they are entitled to an evaluation by alternate means.

are entitled to an equal opportunity to learn. If the location, delivery system, or instructional methodology limits their access, participation, or ability to benefit, they have a right to reasonable alterations in those aspects of the course (or program) to accommodate their disability.

are entitled to an equal opportunity to participate in and benefit from the academic community. This includes access to services, extracurricular activities, housing, and transportation at a comparable level as that provided to any student.

have a right to appeal the institution's decisions concerning accommodations: internally by filing a petition to the _____ committee; externally by filing a complaint with the regional Office of Civil Rights or through the Civil Court system.

INDEX

ABOUT THE CONTRIBUTORS

CHARLES BABB is Instructor in Computer Science and Mathematics at Neosho County Community College, Kansas. He has published articles in *Innovations Abstracts* and the *ESU CIS Newsletter for Two-Year Colleges*. He has been a member of the National Association for Developmental Education since 1981. He has presented at local, regional, and national meetings of developmental educators.

WANDA BAER (Retired) was for ten years the Director of Tutorial Services, a large learning assistance program at Sinclair Community College in Dayton, Ohio, where she worked with students, tutors, and faculty to promote understanding of learning styles, accommodations for learning disabilities, and teaching strategies to facilitate all students in the learning process. She also presented on these topics at state and national conferences. For the past fifteen years, she has worked with the local public access cable channel as an independent producer of over 150 television programs dealing with cultural diversity, humanitarian problems and concerns, education, and health.

JUDY BARNES is a licensed psychologist and instructor at Tyler Junior College (TJC) in Tyler, Texas. She has worked in psychological testing and remediation with learning disabled students for more than 15 years. Recently she has developed an interest in working with the Deaf and has become certified a Sign Language Interpreter. She uses the Sign Language skills as psychologist for the Deaf and as

Director of the Interpreter Training Program at TJC.

BRUCE BARRETT is Coordinator of Academic Services at Kent State University's East Liverpool, Ohio campus. He is a psychologist and a clinical reading specialist, with emphasis in the identification and correction of learning problems. He has worked with high risk student populations of all ages since 1973. For the past fifteen years, he has developed programs designed to enhance the academic success of high risk, college-adult learners, and conducted research in student academic success and retention as related to those programs.

SUSAN BARTZAK-GRAHAM is the Director of the University of Massachusetts Boston's Student Support Services Project, and has served as the Assistant Dean/Director of Academic Advising and Assistance at Wheelock College, and as a Counselor and Acting Director of Counseling and Placement Services at Roxbury Community College. She has worked with traditional and nontraditional students from diverse racial, ethnic and linguistic heritages in the development, implementation, and direct service provision of student advising/counseling and academic support services. She is an adjunct faculty member at Roxbury Community College and the Urban College of Boston in Social Sciences/Human Services. She is also the parent of a child with learning disabilities.

MARY BROWN teaches at Lansing Community College in Michigan.

DEANN CHRISTIANSON is Director of the Mathematics Resource Center at the University of the Pacific in California. She is responsible for a placement testing system, developmental courses, and a tutoring program. Her interests include problems in teaching and learning mathematics, and she also teaches in the Mathematics Department.

DEBORAH J. COCHENER is an Associate Professor of Mathematics in the Developmental Studies Program at Austin Peay State University in Clarksville, Tennessee. She has published articles and presented papers at both state and national conferences on mathematical pedagogy, including the use of graphing calculators. She recently coauthored the ancillary texts *Explorations in Beginning and Intermediate Algebra Using the TI-82, Explorations in College Algebra Using the TI-82/83, with Appendix Notes for the TI-85*, and *Explorations in Precalculus Using the TI-82/83, with Appendix Notes for the TI-85*.

KATHERINE W. CREERY is a longtime instructor in the Developmental Studies Department of the University of Memphis in Tennessee. She has authored articles and presented at state and national levels about practical approaches to overcoming learning disabilities. She brings a wealth of personal experiences to the subject.

JORENE DEAMICIS-BURKE is a Learning Disabilities Specialist with the Disability Resource Center at Ocean County College in Toms River, New Jersey. She has been part of a staff that has made the Ocean County College support program a recognized national model in the field of providing comprehensive services to postsecondary students with special needs. She has spoken at a variety of college conferences within the state on appropriate accommodations for college-capable students with learning disabilities, and on the importance of strategic learning. She has contributed to the *New Jersey Journal of Lifelong Learning* with an article on reading strategies presented to the New Jersey chapter of Literacy Volunteers.

ANDRA DORLAC is the Coordinator of the Learning Skill Center at Lewis and Clark Career Center in St. Charles, Missouri. Her contribution to this publication was drawn from an experience as Associate Professor in the Learning Center at Jefferson College. She has been a special educator, reading specialist, ABE/GED instructor, and private tutor. Her publication of an article on holistic approaches for developmental reading improvement courses resulted from her master's paper and presentation on this topic at a National Association for Developmental Education conference.

MAXINE ELMONT is a professor in Behavioral Sciences at Massachusetts Bay Community College. She has published articles and presented workshops on developmental education, decision making, values clarification, and teaching strategies. Using creative and innovative techniques, she helps individuals strive toward their potential. She serves as a board member and volunteer for many community and professional organizations.

PATRICIA ENEY is a lecturer in English at Miami University Middletown, Ohio. Though this is her first published article, she has been very active in the developmental education field, presenting at several conferences and serving on various committees and boards. Currently, she is working on an article about personalizing the teaching of writing.

JOAN ESSIC is a counselor at the University of North Carolina in Greensboro.

MEREDITH GILDRIE is an Assistant Professor in Reading in the Developmental Studies Program at Austin Peay State University in Clarksville, Tennessee. She also coordinates the reading, study skills, and writing sections of the Program. Her scholarly work has focused on stimulating interest in reading and building background knowledge to facilitate ease of reading.

PAULA GILLS is Director of the Learning Support Center and 504/ADA academic service coordinator at Norwich University in Northfield, Vermont, where she also teaches freshman composition and developmental writing. She has given numerous presentations and workshops on postsecondary learning disability programming and instruction at national and regional conferences such as LDA, CCCC, and the New England affiliate of NADE. She has been published in the Purdue *Writing Lab Newsletter*, *Conversations in Composition*, and the Learning Assistance Association of New England's *Sourcebook for Developmental Educators*.

KAY HARALSON is an Associate Professor of Mathematics in the Developmental Studies Program at Austin Peay State University in Clarksville, Tennessee. She has worked extensively on the use of graphics calculators in developmental mathematics courses. Her interests also include using study skills and writing to enhance the learning of mathematics, and working with students with Attention Deficit Disorder.

JEANNE L. HIGBEE is an Associate Professor in the Counseling Component of the Division of Academic Assistance at the University of Georgia. In addition to writing about students with disabilities, she is the author of numerous articles on affective barriers to academic achievement. She has served as co-editor of the *Selected Conference Papers* and is currently co-editor of the monograph series for the National Association for Developmental Education (NADE). In the past she has served as Associate Editor of the *College Student Affairs Journal* and is now on the American College Personnel Association Media Board.

BONNIE M. HODGE is an Associate Professor of Mathematics in the Developmental Studies Program at Austin Peay State University in Clarksville, Tennessee. She has published articles and presented papers at both state and national conferences on mathematical pedagogy, including the use of graphing calculators. She recently coauthored the ancillary texts *Explorations in Beginning and Intermediate Algebra Using the TI-82*, *Explorations in College Algebra Using the TI-82/83, with Appendix Notes for the TI-85*, and *Explorations in Precalculus Using the TI-82/83, with Appendix Notes for the TI-85*.

SALLIE JOACHIM is an Assistant Professor and the Writing Specialist in the Learning Assistance Center at Hudson Valley Community College (HVCC) in Troy, New York. She is on the Advisory Board for *Research and Testing in Developmental Education*, a publication of the New York State College Learning Skills Association (NYCLSA). She has written book reviews for this publication as well as articles for *Academic Notes*, an annual campus newsletter published by HVCC's School of Liberal Arts and Sciences. She also served as editor for *Noozletter*, NYCLSA's newsletter.

VERDERY B. KENNEDY is Assistant Professor of Learning Support Reading at Georgia Southern University. Her publications include a text for team-taught Developmental Reading and English classes entitled *Reading Writing Relationships*.

Her research interests are in the areas of learning and teaching styles, metacognition, and learning strategies. She is currently participating in a grant program to improve instruction at the university level.

L. SCOTT LISSNER is the Director of Academic and Disabilities Support Services and the ADA/504 Compliance Officer at Longwood College in Virginia. His publications include articles and chapters on accommodation strategies, policy and legal issues related to disability, and a recent chapter on financial trends and the need for change in higher education. He has presented on disability issues at numerous regional and national conferences including The National Association of Developmental Education, The American College Personnel Association, and the National Association of Student Personnel Administrators. He is currently on the executive board of the Virginia Association of Higher Education and Disability, a member of the Task Force on Disability of the American College Personnel Association and President of the Virginia College Learning Association.

ARLENE LUNDQUIST is Coordinator of the Learning Disability Program and the rest of Disabled Student Services at Appalachian State University in Boone, North Carolina. She has held that position for eighteen years. Her professional activities include conference presentations, consulting, and several publications in the area of postsecondary learning disabilities. In addition, she teaches the Introduction to Learning Disabilities course for the College of Education at Appalachian.

MARY MATTSON-SCIROCCO teaches in the Department of Developmental Studies in DeKalb College, Georgia.

CARLA MOLDAVAN is Associate Professor of Mathematical Sciences at Berry College in Rome, Georgia. Previously, she taught at Kennesaw State College, Dalton College, and Murray County High School. Her primary teaching responsibilities have been mathematics courses for teacher education students, developmental studies (learning support) mathematics courses, and general education mathematics courses. She is particularly interested in students' affect toward mathematics and enjoys working with students who consider themselves to not be strong in mathematics.

NANCY POLING was recently a learning specialist in The Learning Center at Roberts Wesleyan College in Rochester, New York. Her job responsibilities included providing assistance to students with disabilities, teaching study skills, and tutoring. She is presently living in Evanston, IL.

JENNIE PRESTON-SABIN is an Associate Professor of Mathematics in the Developmental Studies Program at Austin Peay State University in Clarksville, Tennessee. She is actively involved with the National Association for

Developmental Education and the Tennessee Association for Developmental Association and has published and presented a broad range of topics including providing access for learning mathematics for the underprepared college student and the use of long-term projects to connect algebra to the real world. She has coauthored several testbank ancillaries for prealgebra, elementary algebra, and intermediate algebra and has coauthored *Worksheets and Study Guide for Intermediate Algebra* and *Worksheets and Study Guide for College Algebra*.

JACQUELINE ROBERTSON is coordinator of academic services for students with disabilities at Ball State University in Muncie, Indiana. She is also coordinator of reading and study skills in the Learning Center so many of her publications and presentations have focused on improving academic support to students. She was president of Indiana's chapter of the National Association for Developmental Education and serves on the Indiana Adult Literacy Coalition.

SARI ROSENHECK is Instructor of Standard English at Sullivan County Community College (SCCC) in Loch Sheldrake, New York. She is also the fulltime manager of the Center for Learning Assistance, which coordinates the Tutoring and Academic Support Services offices. She brought the SCCC tutorial program to International Certification through the College Reading and Learning Association. She is the staff advisor for SCCC's writing club, Creative Expressions, and is an active member of the Catskill Reading Society.

KARYN L. SCHULZ is the Coordinator for Learning Disabilities at Essex Community College, in Baltimore, Maryland. She provides academic accommodations for students with disabilities and teaches a college preparation course for students with learning difficulties. Karyn is currently a member of many organizations including AHEAD, LDA, and the membership chair of the Nation's Capital Area Disability Support Services Coalition. Karyn has taken a recent interest and has presented to literacy providers the issues surrounding literacy and learning disabilities.

LYNN SKAGGS is an adjunct instructor at Dodge City Community College, Kansas. She is a reading specialist and a certified English as a Second Language teacher. She holds degrees from Emporia State University and Kansas State University.

MILDRED R. STEELE is an Emerita faculty member of English at Central College in Pella, Iowa. She has just completed a twenty-year study of the lives of fifty-two underprepared freshmen who remained in college. She is a scholar/lecturer for the Iowa Humanities Board (IHB) and has made 50 IHB presentations to date.

NANCY A. STRICKLIN was an Assistant Professor of English at Pellissippi State Technical Community College (PSTCC) in Knoxville, Tennessee, when she implemented the use of tape cassettes in the composition classroom. Dr. Stricklin, who taught at the public high school level as well as college, authored *A Comprehensive Index to Volumes 1 and 2 of E. L. Grigg's Collected Letters of Samuel Taylor Coleridge*, a novel of her own, *The Trust*, and helped develop and publish a literary magazine for college students at PSTCC. A member of MLA and Phi Kappa Phi, she would best be remembered as an author, artist, and one who was keenly interested in her fellow man. Dr. Stricklin died September, 1995.

ELEANOR SYLER, Associate Professor at Evangel College in Springfield, Missouri, is Educational Consultant and lecturer on learning and study skills. She is author of *Study Skills: Good to the Core* and many articles on study techniques, teaching techniques and motivation. She served as President for the Midwest Regional Association for Developmental Education (MRADE). In 1994, she was MRADE's Outstanding Educator of the Year.

ELAINE WERNER is the Associate Coordinator of the Mathematics Resource Center at the University of the Pacific, California. She has published several solutions manuals for developmental mathematics textbooks. Her interests include teaching developmental mathematics to students with learning disabilities.

RECOMMENDED READING AND RESOURCE LIST

EDITOR'S ANNOTATED LIST

A Guide to Reasonable Accommodations for Students with Disabilities (1992), written by L. Scott Lissner, Coordinator of Services for Individuals with Disabilities, The Learning Center, Longwood College, Farmville, VA 23909–1899. Telephone: 1–809–395–2391 or TTY/TDD Relay 800–828–1120. Lissner published a faculty guide on his campus to provide a resource to faculty working with students with disabilities. This guide has been revised and represents an excellent overview on teaching and learning rights and responsibilities at Longwood College.

Assisting College Students with Learning Disabilities: A Tutor's Manual, written by Pamela Adelman and Debbie Olufs for the Association on Handicapped Student Service Programs in Postsecondary Education (AHSSPPE, now AHEAD—see address below). This is a manual designed for tutors working with students with learning disabilities at the college level.

Association on Higher Education and Disability (AHEAD), PO Box 21192, Columbus, OH 43221–0192. Telephone: 614–488–4972 (V/TDD). This association can provide a directory of resources and publications. It publishes a refereed journal called *Journal of Postsecondary Education and Disability.* AHEAD's previous name was the Association on Handicapped Student Service Programs in Postsecondary Education (AHSSPPE).

Faking It: A Look into the Mind of a Creative Learner, written by Christopher Lee and Dr. Rosemary Jackson. It is published by Boynton/Cook Publishers, Heinemann, 361 Hanover Street, Portsmouth, NH 03801-3912. Telephone: 1-800-541-2086. Christopher Lee tells his story of the struggles, challenges, and triumphs that he had while attending The University of Georgia. Lee is now the Director of Training for the Learning Disabilities Research and Training Center located at The University of Georgia, 534 Aderhold Hall, Athens, GA 30602.

Higher Education and the Handicapped Project of the American Council on Education, (HEATH Resource Center), One Dupont Circle, Suite 780, Washington, DC 20036. Telephone: 1-800-544-3284(V/TDD). The *HEATH Resource Directory* and National Resources for Adults with Learning Disabilities are available and bulletins on various topics can be ordered from the HEATH Publications List.

IBM National Support Center for Persons with Disabilities, PO Box 2150, Atlanta, GA 30301-2150. Telephone: 1-800-284-9482. A resource guide can be obtained about assistive technology.

Legal Considerations for Serving Students with Learning Disabilities in Institutions of Higher Education, written by Jeanne M. Kincaid, Esq., 101 Varney Road, Center Barnstead, NH 03225. Telephone: 603-776-5404. Legal publications, like the one listed, which address the needs of students with disabilities in higher education can be obtained directly from Kincaid, who is an Attorney at Law practicing exclusively in the area of disability law.

Project EASI (Educational Access to Software and Information), EDUCOM/EUIT, 1112 16th Street, NW, Suite 600, Washington, DC, 20036. This project is dedicated to helping higher education use computer support for people with disabilities. This support is in the areas of access to information resources, instruction, research, and employment.

Promoting Postsecondary Education for Students with Learning Disabilities, written by Loring C. Brinckerhoff, Stan F. Shaw, and Joan M. McGuire. This is a handbook providing a comprehensive look at services needed for college students with learning disabilities. It can be ordered from PRO-ED, 8700 Shoal Creek Boulevard, Austin, TX 78757.

Recording for the Blind (RFB), 20 Roszel Rd., Princeton, NJ 08540. Telephone: 609-452-0606. Taped educational books can be obtained for people who are unable to read standard print because of a visual, physical, or perceptual disability.

CONTRIBUTORS' LIST

Dollahan, J. (April 1986). "A Guide for Parents of College-bound Learning Disabled High School Students." Position Paper Series, document no. 7. Greenvale, NY: Long Island University Press.

Garnett, K. & La Porta, S. (1991). *Dispelling the Myths: College Students and Learning Disabilities*. (2nd ed.). New York: National Center for Learning Disabilities, Hunter College.

Hallowell, E. & Ratey, J. (1994). *Driven to Distraction*. New York: Pantheon.

Higbee, J. L.(1996). "'Who belongs' versus 'Who gets to stay.'" *Research and Teaching in Developmental Education*, 12(2), 81–86.

Higbee, J. L., Dwinell, P. L., & Kalivoda, K. S. (1989). "Serving Learning Disabled Students Within and Outside the Classroom." (ERIC Document Reproduction Service no. ED 305 869).

Kahn, M. (1980). "Learning Problems of the Secondary and Junior College Learning Disabled Student: Suggested Remedies." *Journal of Learning Disabilities*, 13(8), 445–449.

Kalivoda, K. S. & Higbee, J. L. (1994). "Implementing the Americans with Disabilities Act," *Journal of Humanistic Education and Development*, 32, 133–137.

Kalivoda, K. S. & Higbee, J. L. (1995). "A Theoretical Model for the Prediction of Faculty Intention to Accommodate Disabled Students." *Journal of Educational Opportunity*, 7(1), 7–22.

Kalivoda, K. S. & Higbee, J. L. (1989). "Students with Disabilities in Higher Education: Redefining Access." *Journal of Educational Opportunity*, 4, 14–21.

Mangrum, Charles T. & Strichart, Stephen S. (1984). *College and the Learning Disabled Student—A Guide to Program Selection, Development, and Implementation*. Orlando, FL: Grune & Stratton.

Michaels, C.A. (1988). *How to Succeed in College: A Handbook for Students with Learning Disabilities*. Albertson, NY: Human Resources Center.

Nadeau, K. (1994). *Survival Guide for College Students with ADD or LD*. New York: Magination Press.

Nolting, P. D. (1991). *Math and the Learning Disabled Student: A Practical Guide for Accommodations*. (1st ed.). Pompano Beach, FL: Academic Success Press.

Nolting, P. D. (1991). *Winning at Math*. (2nd ed.). Pompano Beach, FL: Academic Success Press.

Quinn, P. (ed.). (1994). *ADD and the College Student*. New York: Magination Press.

Scheiber, B. & Talpers, J. (1985). *Campus Access for Learning Disabled Students—A Comprehensive Guide*. Washington, DC: Closer Look.

Scheiber, B. & Talpers, J. (1987). *Unlocking Potential: College and Other Choices for Learning Disabled People—A Step-by-Step Guide*. (1st ed.). Bethesda, MD: Alder & Alder.

Vogel, S. A. (1993). *College Students with Learning Disabilities: A Handbook* (4th ed.). Northern Illinois University Press.

Vogel, S. A. & Adelman, P. B. (eds.) (1993). *Success for College Students with Learning Disabilities*. (1st ed.). New York: Springer-Verlag.

Wren, C. & Segal, L. (1985). *College Students with Learning Disabilities: A Student's Perspective*. Chicago: Depaul University Press.

Yellen, A. G. & Yellen, H. L. (1987). *Understanding the Learning Disabled Athlete: A Guide for Parents, Coaches, and Professionals*. Springfield, IL: Charles C. Thomas.

The York Transition Project. (July 1987). *Making Choices: A Handbook for Learning Disabled Young Adults and Their Parents*. Portland, ME: University of Southern Maine Press.

ISBN 0-275-95606-7

HARDCOVER BAR CODE